£ 2.99

C000129984

Praise for *The Sacred Life of Bread*

"The whole world is contained in a loaf of bread—and Meghan Murphy-Gill has captured not just that, but our humanity in her lovely book. Part memoir, part history, part reveling in the beauty of bread, she takes us on a journey that will never let you look at that hotdog bun or dinner roll the same way again."

> —**Alissa Wilkinson**, author of *Salty: Lessons on Eating, Drinking, and Living from Revolutionary Women*

"A thoughtful reflection on the spirituality of bread-making."

> —**Sandor Ellix Katz**, fermentation revivalist and author of *The Art of Fermentation*

"This book will remind any baker that the process of making bread rekindles one's spiritual connection to and consciousness of the world around them."

> —**Ellen King**, co-owner of Hewn Bakery in Evanston, Illinois, and author of *Heritage Baking*

"If you are looking for a perfect read for that quiet period while the dough is rising, pick up *The Sacred Life of Bread*. Murphy-Gill offers reflections on the hidden meaning of ingredients and surprising insights from familiar actions like mixing, kneading, trying a new recipe, and making a sandwich. She manages to achieve something that many writers do not: all of her many personal stories go beyond the autobiographical to illuminate universal truths of genuine depth. Experienced bakers and newbies alike will find something to savor on every page."

—**Fr. Dominic Garramone,** aka
"The Bread Monk," host of *Breaking Bread with Father Dominic*

"I adored and devoured every page of *The Sacred Life of Bread*. Murphy-Gill's reflections, insights, and recipes connecting the spiritual life to the transformative miracle that is bread-baking stoked my hunger for the simple and life-giving nourishments of both kitchen and eucharistic tables. By the end I was craving a cup of tea, fresh-baked bread and butter, and more of Murphy-Gill weaving stories about my favorite topics: food and God."

—**Jennifer Baskerville-Burrows,** bishop of the Episcopal Diocese of Indianapolis and former food magazine writer and blogger

THE SACRED LIFE OF
BREAD

Uncovering the Mystery
of an Ordinary Loaf

THE SACRED LIFE OF
BREAD

Meghan Murphy-Gill

Broadleaf Books
Minneapolis

THE SACRED LIFE OF BREAD
Uncovering the Mystery of an Ordinary Loaf

Cover image: Bread: Shutterstock/Moljavka;
            Wheat: istock/mashuk
Cover design: Michelle Lenger

Print ISBN: 978-1-5064-8223-1
eBook ISBN: 978-1-5064-8224-8

To Albert and Agnes Meehan,
for always believing in me

CONTENTS

FOREWORD

THE ANCIENT TEACHERS (AS ARTICU-
lated by Dante Alighieri in his thirteenth-century
Convivio) taught that all things can be understood
on four levels of meaning (and I paraphrase): the
literal; the poetic or metaphorical; the philosoph-
ical/ethical; and, at its deepest level, the mystical
or anagogic. But, and this is the key, they added
that one can access the deeper levels only by first
understanding the literal. Which is why bread
makes such a wonderful port of entry, as it is
iconically transparent into those deeper levels of
understanding described by Dante as soon as we
make our first actual loaf of bread. Bread makers,
once they experience the literal aspect of it, so

easily fall under its spell and can, then (if they so desire), intuit its metaphoric depths and beyond.

A myriad of such lofty thoughts bubbled in my mind as I read, with great enjoyment, Meghan Murphy-Gill's book, *The Sacred Life of Bread*. One of those thoughts was, "Here is someone who gets it when it comes to the efficacy of metaphors." Having, myself, made a career of riding the metaphorical horse called "bread" for all its worth, I freely admit that Meghan is a person after my own heart.

I familiarly call her Meghan because we've met and corresponded and, through her writings, how familiar she feels. But I should rightly call her the Reverend Meghan Murphy-Gill, as this book is a literary expression and work of her priestly mission to serve God as a mediator between heaven and earth by providing for us the sacraments—the sacred mysteries—of the Church. But this book is also a great read, for a number of reasons, and that is what I want to address in this foreword.

FOREWORD

It is a tricky tightrope walk to mediate between two worlds. The Judeo-Christian tradition is not alone in teaching that God is uncreated, transcendent—in a word, perfect. But though created in the image and likeness of that God, we are nevertheless flawed, imperfect, always in the process of becoming. We grapple with the challenges of life and struggle with emotions, thoughts both healthy and unhealthy, decisions and choices that are often flawed, grief, fear, and elusive joy. We live in the material world yet yearn for the promise of paradise.

No less subject to these human vicissitudes are priests, even though they are often held by many of us to a higher or more ideal standard. But, despite the fact that they are ordained with the privilege of serving at the altar and representing that bridge between two worlds, they too deal with the same existential challenges as we all do, while still required to perform their job of pointing and guiding us toward that for which we yearn.

THE SACRED LIFE OF BREAD

One of the ways they do this, in addition to their primary sacramental work, is by sharing stories, whether from scripture (which provides the ultimate script, the template of templates) or through insights culled from their own lives and experiences from their own tightrope walk. Good storytellers have a knack for taking their listeners and readers on a journey with them; they can cultivate and illuminate what everyday moments present. They unveil a deeper layer of meaning beneath the literal event by grasping its metaphorical possibility, whether intuitively or consciously. To a good storyteller everything is metaphor, and it is through metaphor that a priest—or anyone for that matter—can find meaning and self-discovery in that tightrope walk between heaven and earth.

So, when a person charged with bridging for us the way to a life of deeper meaning can grasp opportunity by describing, as you will see in the following pages, the virtues of properly buttered New England hot dog rolls or how dipping a grilled cheese sandwich into ketchup elevates an already good sandwich into greatness—you know that person grasps the power of metaphor to transform the mundane into the transcendent. The Reverend Meghan and I happen to share a simpatico background of life experiences as fellow bread bakers, wheat gleaners, storytellers, an obsessive love for both great food and also common everyday food (yes, hot dogs and grilled cheese sandwiches!), and, as noted, a love for metaphors.

In the following pages you will read about these and other ruminations that ferment in the mind and heart of the author. Meghan openly shares the challenges of her own journey as an ordinary human trying to do an extraordinary job. She wrestles with issues such as how to live an authentic, meaningful life during this age of inauthenticity (and she wonders what authentic even means), or how to balance a nostalgic longing for the perceived, maybe exaggerated, virtues of the past good old days with the exciting, though sometimes alienating advances of science and technology, or how to witness to and maintain faith in the goodness of God when we (and the Earth) are having a bad day and everyone is watching.

All this grappling finds its focus and perspective through the lens of that workhorse metaphor, bread, and is given voice through a series of reflections and meditations that take us along with her as Meghan navigates through the various levels of understanding in search of her own authenticity. Who knew that bread could be its own Virgil, guiding the author—and us—to those deeper places?

Peter Reinhart,
July 2022, Charlotte, NC

PREFACE

I BAKED MY FIRST LOAF OF BREAD THE first semester of graduate school, some fifteen years ago. After I popped it into the oven during a brief study break, the familiar aroma of the simple blend of yeast and flour and salt and water drifted from the tiny galley kitchen and around the corner to the desk where I sat in the 500-square-foot apartment I shared with my partner. A comforting bouquet of scents—sweet yet not confectionary, rich yet not heavy—quickly filled the modest space with a whispered truth I seemed to have been born already knowing: bread sustains.

I was working on a master's degree in systematic theology, neck deep in texts that pondered the mysteries of life and beyond. My brain struggled to unravel the threads that theologians wove tightly together in complicated theories about God's relationship to humans and to the created world. But the bread needed no text to speak of sacred things. From the oven it told its story of what had been and what was to come. From the cooling rack, it sang in delicate crackles and faint pops as steam escaped and the caramelized crust continued to form. Was this the same song the earth hummed in its nascent state? Did it also sigh with relief as the ground on which we stand cooled and settled?

The scent lingered all afternoon, beguiling me with promises of comfort and satisfaction, of love and community, of things I could not yet put a word to.

Theology, as I was reminded on my first day of my first class at the seminary where I studied, is commonly described as "faith seeking understanding." That resonated with me. I had, after all, enrolled at a seminary exactly because I sought understanding of the faith I'd been born into and still bore.

Growing up Roman Catholic was never a cerebral experience, which is not to say that my family were unquestioning followers of their religion. To be Catholic in my family was, well, to be a member of the family. The two were synonymous. What else would we be? *Catholic* was how we spoke, a language in which "Jesus, Mary, and Joseph" was as much an exclamation of fear, surprise, or exasperation as it was a little litany. *Catholic* was what we did; it meant rituals having more to do with prayers spoken like spells to call back what was lost and blessings to ward away death and sadness. We weren't every-single-Sunday Catholics. We weren't even Christmas and Easter Catholics if Mass interfered with a family gathering.

The faith I grew up in was not intellectual assent to theological formulations or narrow answers to religious questions provided by a catechism. It was, rather, a chain that traveled backward into untold generations and forward to a vision of heaven, of a world redeemed. The faith of my family was the faith of the people from whom we came: Irish Catholics who'd immigrated to Canada and the United States in search of a life's necessity denied them in their own homeland. Starving, they sailed across the Atlantic, the taste of bread on their tongues.

That hunger moored itself in me both spiritually and physically. And throughout my childhood and into my adulthood, a yearning tugged at my heart to seek more understanding of this inheritance of mine. Finally, in my mid-twenties, I had the opportunity to respond to the longing. It was only in hindsight that I realized I simultaneously began to open cookbooks and books on theology. It's not, I believe, mere coincidence that I sat through lectures on Christology, eschatology, and ecclesiology during the week, learning how generations of fellow seekers have mapped their own longings to know the deeper mysteries at the heart of all that is, only to return home and practice the baking of bread. My explorations of theology satisfied my mind. Kneading dough satisfied my body. Together, they could make my spirit soar.

PREFACE

Since that first loaf, many a boule and baguette have emerged from my oven. I've set pans of hot dinner rolls on tables around which friends and family have gathered. I've baked sandwich loaves for my son's school lunches. I even had a pastry phase, during which I entertained thoughts of formalizing my culinary education. Practicing the techniques required to achieve those satisfying flakey layers of croissants and Danishes quickly set me off that plate. Turns out I enjoy eating Viennoiserie much more than making it.

Bread is now a spiritual practice and ongoing pilgrimage for me. More than a hobby to pass the time or satisfy cravings, it bows my bookshelves that sag under the weight of tomes filled with recipes and methods for how to bake the best breads. It has flung me hundreds of miles from my apartment in Chicago to a farm where heirloom wheat grows in Central Michigan. It has sent me to a pizza school in the exurbs of Chicago to meet and bake and drink with a renowned author of some of those books on my shelves.

I've woken before dawn and set out on a cold January morning to snatch the first loaves from the ovens of professional kitchens tucked in the back of cozy bakeries. I've ordered quantities of yeast and flour that made my husband and me snort with laughter when they arrived because where the hell were we going to store it? And I waited expectantly with millions of others who knew the solace baking bread would bring to themselves and their friends, families, and communities during a global health pandemic that plunged the entire world into uncertainty for these simple, *necessary*, staples to become available again.

There are times when my practice is disciplined, when the peanut butter and jelly sandwiches that make up 75 percent of my son's diet (the other 25 percent is grilled cheese) partake of homemade whole wheat bread, baked weekly in my own trusty oven. Sometimes my practice is on a much looser timeline. No-knead loaves emerge every so often, when I can muster the time or energy between work deadlines and

parenting demands. The sourdough starter sits
dormant in the back of the refrigerator waiting
patiently to be revived. Its maintenance has
been sporadically diligent, outright ignored, and
everything in between. Like spiritual disciplines,
whether meditation or prayer, daily Mass or
daily walks, bread is always there, ready for me
to return, even when I am not.

A spirituality of anything invites the adherent
to experience transformation. A spirituality of
bread should therefore demand a transformation not only in the individual but also in how
the individual relates to the community and the
community to itself. To develop a deep spirituality of bread requires an examination and
transformation of the larger system of how
bread comes to be.

But what is a spiritual discipline for someone
uninterested in religious institutions and formal
belief systems? In my thirties, I stepped out of the

Catholic Church and into the Episcopal Church, where I am now a priest. But many of my friends and acquaintances and even family members are confounded that I would call myself a Christian, that I'd name myself among the membership to an institution they know only as, at best, stifling and, at worst, abusive (a judgment on the institutions that call themselves Christian that is certainly earned). Even more perplexing is that I'd choose the path of leadership in that institution. They sometimes say, "It's not for me." One acquaintance who was particularly intrigued by my life's choices once said to me, "Religion has good things to offer, but it's just not my thing." And yet, she regularly reminded me that she's "spiritual," as if confessing a kindred spirit, that she, too, seeks more.

Barbara Brown Taylor has wondered what "spiritual" means to the so-called spiritual-but-not religious. "It may be the name for a longing—for more meaning, more feeling, more connection, more life," she writes. "When I hear people talk about spirituality, that seems to be what they are describing. They know there is more to life than what meets the eye."

The practice of baking and eating bread is one such way that a person of prayer or a person who is prayer-averse can seek more to life. It is in bread, from the moment a single grain is pressed into the soil to the breaking of a loaf at a table where many are gathered to share food and friendship, that I discover again and again more meaning, more feeling, more connection. That bakers who'd slid hundreds of loaves into their ovens to those who'd shaped not a single roll before, turned to bread baking in a time of frightening global crisis speaks to this experience.

And so, if you've baked hundreds of loaves or not one, you're invited into this practice. If you attend weekly services or don't remember the last time you set foot in a sanctuary, you're invited. If you bake once a week or once a year, you're invited. If you are a mystic or a skeptic, you're invited.

The chapters that follow are not about mastering the perfect artisanal loaf. Among them you will not find the keys to developing a discipline to help you achieve any sort of mastery of anything at all. You will find, however, stories steeped in the mysteries of longing and belonging, practice and rest, and transformation. You may even find your own.

SOIL

I AM AN EPISCOPAL PRIEST. WEEK AFTER
week, I make an offering to God on behalf of
an assembly, some of whom believe in a God
Almighty, Father, Son, and Holy Spirit, some of
whom confide to me aren't so sure about God
but like the music and the regularity of our
ritual and the community that church offers. (I
think they're the ones who really get it. We don't
do this church thing because we have all the
answers, we do it because we know we don't.) I
say a prayer as I lift a wafer of bread and thank
God for all of creation: "For through your goodness we have this bread to offer: fruit of the earth
and work of human hands, it will become for us
the bread of life."

THE SACRED LIFE OF BREAD

I've always loved the poetry of this prayer, and long before I was ordained, I would recite it silently from a pew without moving my lips as the priest said the words aloud. The phrase "work of human hands" was for a long time the most meaningful to me. My own human hands know the work of gathering flour, water, salt, and yeast. They know the work of shaping shaggy dough into smooth boules and baguettes, rolls and flatbreads to be baked, broken, and shared. Human hands have been doing that work since well before an ancient group of outcasts and dissenters called themselves Christians. Bread has been fashioned into shapes and then forged in the fire into something not just edible but edifying to the soul, as offerings to the divine since time immemorial.

But I heard the phrase "fruit of the earth" descend like an ethereal descant across my thoughts as I listened to my friend Nurya Love Parish give a talk on fostering connections between Christians, food, and land some years ago. Now I cannot separate the two phrases "fruit of the earth and work of human hands" when I lift an offering of simple bread in an ancient ritual every week. It is a reminder to all of us that the bread we eat, whether at an altar or a kitchen table, does not begin in the hands of a baker or even in the hands of a farmer who sows and harvests the grain. It begins in the soil.

I introduced myself to Nurya after that talk, and she invited me to the farm she founded, Plainsong Farm in Rockford, Michigan, to plant wheat that would be grown and milled for communion bread guilds. I wake my family on a crisp fall morning before the sun breaks over the horizon and set out on the nearly four-hour drive from Chicago.

It all seems too ordinary when we finally arrive. I had envisioned a bucolic scene: a quintessential farmhouse with black shutters, a long dirt road that cut like the path of an arrow through the fields from a paved road to a house. I had expected bronze cows and spotted cows, speckling the green landscape. I had imagined a patchwork quilt of land spread from here to the horizon.

It's not that I'd never been anywhere rural. It's not even that I'd never been to a farm. Having spent a year and a half as a campus minister, I'd taken a handful of college students gleaning to learn a thing or two about food waste and farm labor. We'd read from the book of Ruth, and I invited them to participate in the ancient tradition of gathering the leftover fruits of a farmer's labor. At a farm in northern Illinois, we picked plump red tomatoes bursting at their own seams and corn so sweet you could eat it raw.

I'd also crossed the country by car more times than I can count, beginning with the drive from New Hampshire to our new home in California when I was ten. I'd sailed the ribbons of highway across wide swaths of verdant, hilly, flat, and parched farmland. Peered at it from thirty thousand feet above on yearly cross-country flights.

But this farm in Central Michigan, just outside Grand Rapids, to where I have made a pilgrimage on a crisp, sun-bright fall day, is smaller than I'd imagined. Ordinary. *Plainsong Farm*, the sign says. *Appropriate*, I think.

And then, *This is a farm?* Where is the great white farmhouse with a wraparound porch? Where is the long dirt road? Where is the farmer in the dell? And his wife and child and their litany of farm animals, cow and pig and chicken? At first sight, this farm is just so, well, plain. As in absolutely normal. As in commonplace. Mundane, even. A house right off the highway. A few cars in the gravel driveway. Neighbors a stone's throw in either direction cast from a strong arm.

The farmhouse is white, and there is a farmer and another farmer, married to each other. They are my age, rounding the turn on middle-aged but still fresh-faced. The apples of their cheeks and smooth steppe of their foreheads not yet leathered by long days in the blazing sun. Their speech tinged with neither twang nor drawl but gilded only slightly by the flat *a* of the Midwest. One of the farmers, Bethany, is an artist and a mother to two sweet children, one a daughter who is the same age as my son. She works part time as a bartender at a brewpub in town.

THE SACRED LIFE OF BREAD

I quickly realize that my notion of farmland and the farmers who tend to it is thanks to the expansive vistas of corn and soybeans seen on those cross-country road trips. My imagination has taken its cues from TV advertisements for American-made cars and patriotic song lyrics about waves of amber grain—self-perpetuating myths of self-reliance and hand-milked cows at dawn.

Here, however, is not a myth. It is the real thing. There is enough land here for a small, diverse crop of vegetables and some chickens. It's not enough to feed America from some proverbial breadbasket but enough to put to use for the growing and raising of food for family and more than several neighbors. It is more than enough. Here is a living memory of a bygone era of small family farms and tiny towns—not poor but not wealthy either—when bellies were filled and bodies were nourished with food that was grown and raised on the same land they woke up on every day.

Nurya believes that everyone, but white Christians of European descent especially, needs to reconnect with the soil in order to engage in the work of confronting a history of dominance and subjugation of people and property. By reconnecting with the land, we can all respond with more empathy to the needs of those who are hungry more efficiently and with more attentiveness to how our use of the land for current needs affects not only the land of the future but those who will need it to continue to fill their bellies. Just look at the past to see how it affects us now. This land was once called home by the Hopewell, Mascouten, and Ottawa tribes, the source of their food, their bread. Now, a group of mostly white Christians come to sow wheat for their communion bread in hopes of discovering pathways to repentance and reconciliation.

The communion wheat program was inspired by the work of another Episcopal priest, Elizabeth De Ruff, who founded a farm and mill in Marin County, California, where heirloom wheat is planted, grown, harvested, and then milled into flour, which is then purchased by local altar bread guilds and shoppers at farmers markets. At

Plainsong, prior to the COVID-19 pandemic, the crop of wheat from the previous year would be milled into flour and then distributed to humble altar bread guilds to be baked into their communion bread. (That program is currently being revived.)

Reconnecting with the soil as a source of bread that the church calls special in some way can help us understand our own place in the vastness of the natural world. Across many cultures can be found creation myths in which human life begins as clay or as dirt. According to the creation myths of Genesis, soil is where all life on earth begins. God separates the Land from the Sea and beckons the earth to put forth vegetation that bears seed as plants and fruit trees. Later, the Creator calls from the land "cattle and creeping things and wild animals of every kind." Likewise, and finally, humankind is called forth. There are two myths of creation told in Genesis, and it's in the second one where God most explicitly calls a human from the soil. God fashions Adam, whose name in Hebrew means "from dirt." It's not just Hebrew, however, that acknowledges etymologically a spiritual connection to the soil. The Latin root of human, *humus*, means soil, dirt, ground.

Despite all the harmful interpretations of Genesis's creation myths that have prevailed for the whole of Western church history, and despite the injustices and misery they have wrought on women, the earth, and anyone who doesn't identify as cisgender, binary, or heterosexual, the heart of the text still moves me. It is a narrative that tells of a common heritage of plants and animals in all their variety. A narrative that tells of a common heritage of humankind in all its variety. Our life here on earth is one *of* the earth. We are made of the same stuff that makes the earth. All of us. Not a one unique. There are no outcasts or misfits among us. The scientific data that came along later confirms the impulses of the earth's early storytellers (and not just of Judeo-Christian origin). All living creatures share DNA. Any two human beings are 99.9 percent genetically identical.

But soil is not just where life begins. Earthly life ends in the soil too. Chicago artist Molly Costello, whose studio is in my neighborhood, goes even further. She sells pins that proclaim, "We are all temporarily not dirt" in casual, stark-white text across a black background, with a shooting star or two above and below. We come from the soil because we are of the same matter as the soil.

I bought one of those pins at the beginning of the COVID-19 pandemic and stuck it to my jacket. The stark reminder was oddly comforting. I had been unmoored by the sudden shutting down of, well, everything. The tethers that had once secured me to a routine existence had been severed, and I felt as if I were floating in a thick mist, barely able to discern the features of a life I once had. I was hovering above that life, my feet no longer able to touch the ground, the soil. The cloud of uncertainty became only thicker as time wore on and obscured not only what I thought I had always known but even what I could hope for. I couldn't see past the days, the hours, the seconds.

SOIL

My son's kindergarten year was cut short, followed by a strange and frustrating year of first grade in which he learned over a computer at home from September to April until he could return for two days a week for the last quarter of the school year. My husband was laid off from a job he'd held for fourteen years, when we were already cash strapped because I was in the process of meeting requirements for ordination. I'd also just started working as a hospital chaplain in January—at a hospital world-renowned for its study of infectious diseases.

I stuck Molly Costello's pin to my jacket not because I like to garden but because "We are all temporarily not dirt" is a blunt reminder of a truth I needed reminding: we earthlings are a community of people and plants, insects and birds. Our earthly existence as many of us live it now is so removed from the earth that it's a wonder that we don't all float away, drifting off into the earth's atmosphere and beyond.

It is in the dirt, from which life emerges and to which it returns, that we experience more.

Elizabeth Johnson, a Catholic feminist theologian, writes, "Rather than being a barrier that distances us from the divine, the matter of this world can function as a mediation to the immediacy of God." The dirt can remind us of the nearness of God, in the places of joy and new life, and also of pain, suffering, death. Acknowledging that *we*, and not just *those other people*, are temporarily not dirt forces us to recognize that we are in this life, on this earth, of this earth, together. And that demands something more from us.

In the Christian tradition, the idea that "we're all temporarily not dirt" runs through our spiritual history. Scripture is filled with stories of prophets who mark themselves with ash and wear sackcloth when their people have rejected the idea that we're all connected and instead start thinking of themselves as God-like, having disposed of the very idea of love because of how it gets in the way of their desire for power and dominance.

SOIL

In hospitals, cleanliness is indeed godliness. I learned this while serving as a chaplain. Sanitation protocols are rigid and necessary for the health and safety of staff and patients. In other words, everything possible is done to protect against "dirt." Hand sanitizing stations outside every room. Clearly marked receptacles for the disposal of anything that has touched or pierced a patient. Sinks and soaps, and yes, masks for everyone now. All to keep the dirt away.

And yet, Ash Wednesday is one of the busiest days of the year. In 2020, it fell not two weeks before the World Health Organization officially declared a global health pandemic. Nurses, doctors, and hospital staff all lined up to see me when I arrived on their floors, a small glass vial of ashes in the pocket of my crisp, white lab coat. I'd stirred the ashes with fragrant frankincense-scented holy oil so the ashes would stick to the foreheads of everyone who asked for them. "From dust you came, to dust you shall return," I intoned, over and over again.

The patients responded to my knocks on their doors. On a normal day, just a handful of patients invited me in when I would stick my head into their rooms and ask, "Is now a good time for a visit?" On Ash Wednesday, nearly everyone invited me in. Over and over, my thumbs traced the sign of a cross onto the foreheads of patients and caregivers, on doctors, nurses, and the patient techs who do the crucial yet unseen work of changing bed linens and delivering hot meals. It is one of the last times I was allowed to use human touch in my spiritual care of the sick that year. Later I wondered if I wasn't anointing them all with dust in preparation for what was to befall us all.

The ashes, the dirt, the dust are powerful. They are mysteriously so. My colleagues and I ponder every year in sermons and planning meetings why the mark of ashes that reminds us of our inevitable death every year is something so many seek out. Ash Wednesday, contrary to popular belief, may be a holy day for those who get ashes., but it is not a Holy Day. Why not come for our more festive celebrations or an easy Sunday service followed by a lemonade and a chocolate chip cookie in the fellowship hall after church? Why the mark of death? Even more, why so public a mark?

I think the book of Jonah (he of "and the Whale" fame) has something to offer. In this story, Jonah arrives in the town of Nineveh to hold a mirror to its people and calls them out for their self-righteousness and greed. Rarely do the accused look at themselves and heed a prophet's message, but in this story the people of Nineveh do just that. But they don't just agree to do better or even to change their behavior, to give up chocolate for forty days or to say a prayer daily. As a community, they take on the spiritual work of transformation by proclaiming a fast and joining together, everyone great and small, in putting on sackcloth and ashes. Even the king. Even the animals. The entire community of Nineveh repents. Whenever I read this story, I think about those ashes, dirt smeared even onto the faces of the animals to remind the entire community that they are in this together. No one, not even a single animal, is spared.

I think that people come out of the woodwork for Ash Wednesday, even in a hospital, whether they lie dying or surround a beloved one on their way out of this life, because we know intuitively, at that soul-deep level, that we are called to the dirt, to the soil. We come from it. The soil is where we bury the dead. The soil is also where we plant the seeds of life. It is a place of beginning and it is a place of our ending, and when we tend to it closely and with reverence, we can know more intimately what it is to live in the presence of something holy. When we press our fingers into the dirt, we press against the edges of our understanding and into the mysterious source of all things.

The Ash Wednesday phenomenon has an interesting contour in a hospital setting when death already draws so much nearer. Those edges are especially sharp in a hospice unit, where I was assigned to distribute ashes in 2020. Death there doesn't just draw near. In some rooms, it is already passing over.

SOIL

It seems so counterintuitive to mark the dying with the sign of their death when death is but hours away, already present in the rattle of their lungs as they take their last breaths. I visited a young woman whose family had requested my presence. Her skin was cool, and though she was actively dying, it was still plump with youth. I traced the sign of the cross on her forehead, leaving a trail of ashes in the wake of my thumb. I did the same on the papery thin skin of her grandmother. Then I moved on to her middle-age uncles and aunts, her teenage sisters and twenty-something cousins. Even the hospice nurse who witnesses death daily came to me. *What does she need reminding for?* I wondered to myself. I, too, bore the mark of death on my own forehead. A sign, in dirt, that we are all in the process of returning to our humble origins, the source of life.

At Plainsong, Bethany's husband, Mike, has prepared the wheat field for us volunteer planters.

He has tilled the soil and marked the rows where we will drop the seeds. Before we get to planting, we pray a blessing over the soil, led by Nurya.

So often, Christian prayer can feel like making a wish, sending it aloft, tied to a balloon in hopes that God, up on his cloud (because in this version, God is often he), will catch it and decide whether to grant it. I know why people pray this way. I even pray this way sometimes. But this prayer over the soil isn't one of those prayers. Instead, it is a simple expression of gratitude. We simply say thank you for the dirt. We thank the dirt itself for being a place where we can plant what we hope will become spiritual as well as physical sustenance. We lay our hands on the soil, not to imbue our own sense of holiness into it, as if we are not ourselves "temporarily not dirt." Rather, we ask the soil, where the wheat that will become the bread of life will soon grow, to change us. And then, we don't send these hopes aloft but push them into the soil.

By the time we've arrived back in the city, under the soil an alarm clock begins to blare, signaling to the wheat berries that it is time. Time to wake up! Time to tap into their own stored memory. Water and warmth jostles awake the dormant embryos inside the seeds, tells them to start feeding on the sugars inside the hull. Soon, they will send their tender shoots upward, reaching for that source of warmth. At the same time, they will begin to push their roots into the soil in search of the water that has been promised. The seeds will begin to germinate, transforming from wheat berries into wheat that will become bread.

SIMPLE DINNER ROLLS

Adapted from *The Joy of Cooking*

Makes 24 rolls

Rare is the reception or party held in celebration of life where a dinner roll of some sort is not served alongside the trays of braised meats, sliced cheeses, and cooked vegetables. These dinner rolls are at once celebratory and comforting, appropriate for baby showers and funerals and every gathering in between.

1 cup (120 g) milk

2 tablespoons (28 g) butter, softened

1 tablespoon (12 g) sugar

¾ teaspoon (4 g) salt

1½ (5 g) instant dry yeast

3½ to 3⅔ cups (420 to 440 g)
all-purpose flour

melted butter for brushing on top of dough
and rolls

1. In a medium bowl, stir together the milk, softened butter, sugar, and salt until the sugar is dissolved. Add the yeast. Place the flour in a large bowl and then add the milk mixture. Combine until the dough comes together. Then knead on a lightly oiled surface until the dough is smooth and pliable, only adding a little more flour if the dough is too wet. Shape into a large ball, place in a lightly oiled bowl, and brush with melted butter.

Cover with a damp cloth or plastic wrap and allow to rise until doubled in size.

2. When the dough is ready, divide it into 30 equally sized pieces. For precision, weigh the dough and divide by 30 and portion out the dough as appropriate. Then, form your hand into a C-shape (or backward C if using your right hand) and roll the pieces into balls, forming a tight skin on the top. Place the portions onto two baking sheets lined with parchment (or lightly oiled) about 2 inches apart. Cover lightly and allow to proof for about 30 to 40 minutes.

3. Meanwhile, preheat the oven to 425°F. When the rolls are light and puffy, bake for 15 minutes or until the tops are golden brown. If you prefer a crisper exterior, remove them to a rack and cool. If you prefer a softer roll, leave the rolls on the pans and brush with melted butter. Cover with clean dish towels for 15 minutes and then remove to a rack to cool.

INACTIVE TIME

I LAUGH WHENEVER I READ A RECIPE that indicates "inactive" time, especially when it's a recipe for bread. As if the only active time is when I am in the kitchen, measuring flour, yeast, water, and salt into my large, metal "baking bowl" (as I call it) that I bought for a few bucks at IKEA. Or kneading it all together into a smooth, pliable dough. Or shaping the dough into its final, to-be baked form.

Yes, I suppose that when I am baking, I am especially active when the dough is in my hands. But when it is left to rest is when the real magic starts to happen. Strands of gluten, formed by kneading, begin to relax. I always imagine this process occurring in the same way my muscles unravel when I lie on the warm sand on the first good and hot day of summer or when I trek to a nearby Korean spa in the depths of winter and thaw out on a straw mat in a sauna so warm the floor is nearly too hot to walk on. If the strands of gluten don't get time to relax, the dough is difficult to work with. You cannot see the strands of protein molecules, but you can certainly feel the effects of them when they get tightly bound. The key is to stop kneading the dough, to stop poking it and prodding it, and just let it rest. Give it time. Then it will work with you.

People can be like this too, can't they? I've sat through enough staff meetings in both secular and supposedly sacred workplaces to know that stressed and overworked coworkers are rarely willing to work with you. I've witnessed months and months of hard work get lost in an instant simply because people were too tired. I've also been a parent long enough to know that the only way to get a wailing child to reason with you (or at least the closest thing to it) is to stop asking questions or making demands and just offer a hug, letting them rest in your arms for a bit. I would never call this time "inactive." All the good things happen during the resting period.

There is no getting around ample time for resting in baking. When I watch *The Great British Bake Off* and see a contestant tell the cameras they're "knocking the temp up a bit" to get bread to proof or rise more quickly, I always cringe. A dough that rises too fast, thanks to too warm conditions or too much yeast, will become slack and bland because the yeast, having consumed too much sugar too quickly, burn out. Think of one-hit-wonder stars or child actors propelled into the spotlight before they've had any time to develop the depth that would sustain a longer career.

The addition of salt to a bread dough is one way to prevent burnout because, in addition to enhancing flavor, it slows down the fermentation process and prevents overproofing. Salt tempers too swift a progress into something more sustainable so that by the time the bread is ready to go into the oven, the yeast offer their last effort in a fitful fury and fermentation finally stops. Timed correctly, yeast peter out just about when it's too hot to survive, providing that "oven spring" that gives bread that glorious, puffed-up look.

Some traditional breads are made without salt. Pane Toscano, for example, was born of a tradition of bread baking during a period of high taxation on salt during the Middle Ages. Bakers adjusted accordingly, and although salt is now more affordable and accessible, the tradition of salt-free baking carries on. This method takes into account the lack of salt and adjusts for proofing time accordingly. I think of gymnasts and ballet dancers, who, accounting for their art's and sport's demands on their bodies, plan their careers accordingly by retiring early. Pane Toscano is often served with highly flavorful dishes. Once stale, it provides the heft of a panzanella, a summer salad of ripe, juicy tomatoes, licorice-like basil, fruity olive oil, bright and acidic vinegar, and, of course, salt. The bread soaks in the flavors of the food it is served with.

Baking bread calls for significant waiting periods, when the dough changes in ways imperceptible to the naked eye at a molecular level. Fermentation occurs when the dough is fully alive. Yeast and bacteria feed in a frenzy on the flour's starch, releasing alcohol and carbon dioxide that, respectively, aid in flavor and rise. We may notice only after the passage of time, in how the dough grows in size, the results of this flurry of activity below the surface, yet we cannot see with our eyes the true work taking place. But the baker can participate in it by allowing that time to pass without getting too involved—perhaps even by resting herself.

On the best kind of baking day—usually one that is dark, damp, and cold, and when there's not much else to do—I will sit in my favorite armchair with a cup of tea, prop up my feet, and read a book. Most baking days, however, require that I "multitask," which usually involves cleaning or catching up on something boring, like email. Ironically, it's the experience of reading, feet propped up, when I am keenly aware of an unfurling in my heart and mind. I become more aware of the world around me, more perceptive of the needs of others, and have more patience for them as well. It is if something very important is happening below the surface, something imperceptible to the naked eye is making me more alive.

This is what I like to think of as "God's time," a phrase beloved of church people. Unfortunately, its meaning gets distorted to convey the protracted passage of time necessary to achieve an end. Sometimes, that distortion can be helpful. This alternative timeline encourages patience when it seems nothing is happening, or worse, that things are declining or getting worse, as if a series of defeats mean the war is lost. God's time is the space through which Martin Luther King's long arc of justice travels, so chin up, not all is lost. Progress is not always linear.

But the phrase also covers a multitude of sins, particularly as they relate to inefficient time management or lack of courage and leadership to change. "Yes, change is important, but it must happen on God's time," says a council of bishops. Religious institutions don't suffer alone from a misunderstanding of God's time. Any large institution with humans at the helm can easily fall into the do-nothing trap, either kicking a proverbial can down the road for later leadership to handle or resisting progress at all costs and blaming the stagnation on the need for more time. It is possible to oversalt bread dough and kill the yeast. There is a difference between rest and stagnation, one of which is deadly. In my own process of becoming a priest, I heard the phrase "God's time" uttered so often, I started to wonder whether my file had fallen behind a cabinet somewhere and "God's time" simply referred to the amount of time it was taking to find it. Or maybe God had forgotten about me. I felt incredibly salty.

Jesus endured a waiting period, a feature of those forty days Christians mark in the season of Lent I only recognized while enduring my own extended waiting period. In three gospel stories, Jesus endures forty days of fasting, temptation, prayer, and solitude in the desert before embarking on a public ministry to turn the world upside

down. How else does one look into the faces of
leaders political and religious proclaiming, "The
first shall be the last," without spending some
time in preparation? I can't prepare a sermon to
proclaim to fellow believers without first spending several hours in reflection.

There is a danger in speaking of God's time
just as there is danger in speaking about God at
all. For when we start attributing characteristics
to the divine in order to explain things about
our own lives, whether good or lacking, we risk
turning the divine into something we can hold in
our back pocket, like a card we can pull out and
wave as an excuse for our shortcomings. How
often we limit God in this way. Just because God
is eternal and infinite does not mean that God
is a woefully inefficient manager of time. And
yet, I certainly hope that God is not nearly as
concerned with efficient time management as I
can be.

A way to glean insight into "God's time" is to
observe the natural world and our everyday experiences, which offer a glimpse into not so much

the length of God's time but the possibilities born within it. In God's time a series of chemical reactions sparked fifteen billion years ago resulted in a multitude of flora and fauna that now populate the earth and the lives of which are inextricably connected. But God's time is not always measured in eons. In God's time a young mind experiences a flash of insight and understanding after having been read to for five or six years, and a child is able to decipher the lines and curves on a page into letters, words, sentences. Suddenly, entire worlds are cracked open, and a lifetime of discoveries lies ahead.

Bread becomes bread in God's time, a cycle that starts in the soil as grain tucked in to rest in a loamy bed. Shortly after a fall planting of winter wheat, before the cold settles in for a season, the wheat kernel absorbs moisture and begins to ready itself for spring, that season of verdancy when everything that has been in a deep sleep, snug under blankets of soil and snow, suddenly bursts with life and activity. The process, *vernalization*, is even named for the springtime, a sort of leap of faith that it will indeed survive the winter. And not just survive but, when the earth has thawed, reproduce. Vernalization is how the seed prepares for reproduction. When spring comes, the seed will produce more than the blades of vegetation as long as vernalization has occurred. It will produce fiftyfold—but it must first experience the cold. Without the drop in temperature, the plant will not flower come spring.

Wheat farmers are particularly dependent on this process. Vernalization is how the seeds resist damage from winter's frost and what ensures a crop that can be harvested for the grain, ever more kernels of wheat to become feed for animals, planted for new crops of wheat, or milled into flour for bread. Vernalization makes food possible, several seasons in advance.

Even before vernalization, a kernel of wheat germinates. Nestled in the soil, it absorbs moisture, which helps convert the carbohydrates that surround the seed's germ into energy that it will consume as it shoots out of the seed and into the soil. Once exposed to the cold, however, that process stops and the kernel prepares for its winter rest.

I'm reminded of what I often hear called "the incubation period" in the creative process, whether for writing, painting, or composing music. Often, an artist experiences a burst of energy for a project and then needs to "put it to bed" for a time before getting back to creating. The shape of the creative process often includes an initial flare of energy followed by a fallow period when it seems as if the project will die (and sometimes, it actually does). But after wintering over, if the project is to flourish, there is new growth, signs of life. And so begins the growing season in which the project is tended to, little by little, until it is finally ready to harvest.

"Transformation is the business of winter," writes Katherine May in *Wintering*, a lyrical meditation on a season too often associated with death and dormancy. Life goes on in winter, even if not in the productive manner we expect of the rest of the year. It is the life cycle's crucible,

43

writes May. Indeed, its blanket of snow ensures a restful sleep for a field planted with wheat. The frosty layer nurtures the health and strength of the grasses that will eventually grow once the soil has softened under the spring sun. Transformation is the invisible flurry of activity below the surface, a reorganizing at a cellular or soul-deep level, a renewing, a conversion of one thing into another. It is the unfurling of possibility, the slow uncovering of the previously unimaginable. Transformation is the business of God's time.

NO-KNEAD RYE BREAD

Adapted from *My Bread* by Jim Lahey

The first rise of any no-knead, artisan-style bread requires a long waiting period of 12 to 18 hours to develop flavor. In this version, rye flour, just a quarter of the total amount of flour, increases the flavor. Caraway seeds are optional but give the bread recognizable deli rye flavor.

2¼ cups (300 g) bread flour

¾ cup (100 g) rye flour, plus additional for dusting

1¼ teaspoons (8 g) table salt

½ teaspoon (2 g) instant dry yeast

1⅓ cups (300 g) cool water

1½ teaspoons (9 g) caraway seeds (optional)

1. In a medium bowl, combine the flours, salt, and yeast. Add the water and mix into a sticky dough, using your hand, wooden spoon, or dough whisk. Cover the bowl with plastic wrap and let rise at room temperature for 12 to 18 hours. The surface will be dotted with bubbles and the dough will have more than doubled in size when it's ready. Alternatively, cover the dough and allow it to rise in the refrigerator for at least 24 hours.

Bring it to room temperature before moving ahead.

2. When the dough is ready, dust a work surface with flour and tip out the dough, using a spatula or bowl scraper to ease it all out in one piece. Gently, with floured hands, shape the dough, which will be quite blob-like at this point, into a round by lifting the edges and pulling them toward the center. Carefully turn it over, seam-side down, and tuck in and under the edges. Drape a large tea towel into a medium-sized bowl or a proofing basket and dust it generously with flour. Transfer the dough seam-side down to the bowl or basket. Sprinkle the top with flour and fold the tea towel to loosely cover it. Allow to rise for 1 to 2 hours. It is ready when it no longer springs back when poked.

3. Meanwhile, at least a half hour before baking, preheat the oven to 475°F with a rack in the lower third and place a Dutch

oven or another heavy pot with a cover in the center of the rack.

4. Carefully remove the Dutch oven once preheated and uncover it. Gently tip the dough, seam-side up this time, into the pot and quickly cover with the lid. Bake for 30 minutes with the lid on. Remove the lid and bake 15 to 30 more, or until the bread is deeply browned but not burned.

5. Remove the loaf carefully to a rack to cook. It is essential to wait until the bread is completely cool before slicing.

PRAYER

THE MORE BOLDLY A BREAD RECIPE
boasts a perfect outcome, the more likely it's all
wrong. Every loaf is a leap of faith, and trying to
follow the recipe with exactitude, in hopes that
doing so will guarantee a particular, repeatable
outcome, will only lead to despair. Even if you
do manage to slavishly follow a recipe's steps, so
many other variables go into a loaf: the temperature of the room, the humidity of the air, even
the mood of the baker.

This is not to say that bread recipes should
not be written or followed. In my own baking,
I stick with a few favored recipes. But they serve
more like guidelines than an exact script. I'll
leave open a couple of preferred bread books

on the counter for a few days and flip through the pages as I make my way through a baking day. Claire Saffitz's guide to sourdough on the *New York Times* Cooking page is another go-to, and I'll scroll through her suggestions, using my elbow or the back of my wrist so as not to get bread dough or flour into the keyboard. Fifteen years of bread baking and I still need reminders on the timing of a rise or the method for adding salt to a dough of just flour and water during the autolyse phase. And so, I read recipes.

Using exact measurements of weight and volume will not result in the perfect loaf of bread, no matter what the latest "definitive" guide to bread baking says. Even if you weigh your ingredients to the exact tenth of a gram. Even if you bake at precisely the recommended temperature in an oven that has been calibrated to the exact tenth of a degree. Even if you use the same brand of flour and yeast your favorite Instagram bread guru has suggested (and likely been given by said brands).

PRAYER

If there is a problem with bread recipes, it is that they rarely account for context. A recipe has captured the conditions of a particular moment in time. The humidity might be particularly high and air temperature particularly cool. The age, and not just the brand, of the yeast makes a difference. The wild yeasts of the air may be especially exuberant, such as in my own kitchen, where my husband regularly brews kombucha and makes yogurt, indirectly coaxing the bread dough I prepare into loaves that rise with ease. Or if the recipe was created and tested in a sterile kitchen, wild yeast may be nonexistent.

Some recipes are indeed very reliable, but even the most seasoned recipe developers I know admit that when on a deadline for a book that is contracted to have fifty different recipes, a good chunk go untested and are based on instinct alone. And then there are the recipes I know just by glancing at them that will never work. They may promise that great and wonderful things will happen in your life if you just use these ingredients, in this way, but those promises are empty and will only make you feel as if you've failed.

Recipes are best when approached like written prayers found in a prayerbook. They offer insight into a practice but never promise mastery. They can capture someone else's idea or give us something to call back from our distant memory, collective or individual. They can connect us to someone else's innovative method or to a tried-and-true tradition. They can inspire us to try something new—or remind us that there are some methods that just don't work anymore.

New bakers, especially, really need recipes. Without them, how would you even know where to begin? How would you know the ratio of flour to water necessary for a chewy center and robust crust or at what temperature to bake your baguettes? A vague method is not likely to turn a new baker into an accomplished one. Recipes initiate bakers into the world of bread. They etch the patterns of bread baking into their being. From there they can go exploring.

Set prayers, I often think—the prayers I find
in the prayerbooks that line some of my bookshelves and sit in stacks atop my desk—are to
God what recipes are to bread. They etch patterns from which one can later explore and to
which one can return again and again. One of
the reasons my generation finds it so difficult to
not only speak to God but of God is that we were
the first generation to be raised by predominantly
religiously indifferent parents or parents who, in
reaction to the strict formulas of their parents'
faith, opted out completely. Our parents claimed
that by not instilling a particular faith, we would
have the opportunity to figure out our religious
identity on our own, therefore making it more
meaningful to us. We could determine what we
wanted, not what our parents wanted, by the
time we became adults.

But we weren't given the words to practice
speaking plainly and with confidence to God. We
were told that prayers don't work or that they were
silly and too simple. In the Christian tradition,
"Now I lay me down to sleep" are pretty good,

albeit simple, words for a child becoming aware of their own mortality. "Give us our daily bread" is slightly more complicated but orients the heart toward goodness. The words of Mary, mother of Jesus, "My soul doth magnify the Lord," are even more complex. Her sudden eruption of joy at the announcement of an impossible pregnancy offers a way to express the mix of emotions when we encounter the wildly unexpected presence of God. These old words, maybe not our own, are grooves in old stones in which we can trace our fingertip. Old words to start with and return to when we don't know what else to say to God or we simply need to connect with another's capacity to speak of holy things, are a way to encounter what we hold sacred. The point here is to practice the patterns, not to master them.

Bakers know the patterns—mix, knead, rise, knead again, shape, rise, bake, cool, eat. It's the particularities that change. I know bakers who bake by muscle memory. I do not. I need regular reminders of what to do next. I still struggle with oven spring. I've yet to figure out exactly what works for getting the yeast to proof just enough before it goes into the oven so that it releases a last gasp in those high temperatures, creating those larger, more erratic holes typical of rustic artisan breads. I have used the stretch and fold method of creating strong gluten strands rather than kneading and ended up overworking the dough before it even reached that all-important stage when you can stretch a piece of it thin enough to see light through it. I've also given up on reaching that stage only to bake bread that turned out delicious and with a chew.

My scoring needs work—those confident slashes to allow the bread room to rise in the oven don't always look so confident in my hand. Sometimes they are over confident. Or messy. Or I forget them. I also have yet to figure out if I should bake my loaves directly from the refrigerator as one of my trusted resources says to do, or bring them to room temperature first, allowing them to puff up a bit more, before popping them into the oven. I've tried both. And both have succeeded. And both have failed.

THE SACRED LIFE OF BREAD

A friend of mine often asks for suggestions. She will text when she's in the middle of baking and needs help troubleshooting various snafus: bread that tends to stick to her Dutch oven, proofing in a cold kitchen, bread that won't proof. My answer is not unlike the answer we Episcopalians offer when someone asks us what specifically we believe about x or y or z. "It depends," I say. What does it depend on? Your intent, whom you ask, what is happening in the room.

Despite my collection of many wonderful recipes, I've never baked a perfect loaf of bread. There's always something I could have done better or need more of or need less of. More color on the crust. Better scoring. More rise. Less tang. More moisture. Less moisture. Better crumb structure. And save for a few real doozies that had to be thrown like bricks into the compost bucket, every single one of those imperfect loaves has been eaten. Toasted and spread with butter or slathered in jam. Drizzled with honey. Topped with mashed avocado. Dipped into soups. Swiped across the last of the sauce on a dinner plate.

Layered with cheese and grilled. Pulled in chunks to be eaten plain. Those supposedly imperfect, nonmasterful loaves have turned out not just edible but perfectly enjoyable.

Few things are written in stone when it comes to bread baking. Despite how book after book promises perfect loaves if you just follow these recipes or these methods. Despite the frequency of the word *master* in too many titles, bidding you to come and "master the art of bread." As if it could ever be mastered. On my kitchen shelf is a particularly confident title, *The Bread Bible*. But perhaps it is actually a more appropriate way to approach baking: growing in wisdom by telling and listening to and wrestling with stories shared across the ages.

My refusal to acknowledge mastery of anything and rather approach everything from prayer to bread making as engaging with the mystery of the universe has earned me some skeptics. Young men in particular have told me they think I avoid answering questions about the essential nature of God by inviting them to rethink the nature of their question. What some call an agnostic approach to faith is the only way I can have a faith that is honest, about God, about the deepest mysteries of life and the universe, about yeast, and flour, and the soil, and heat. I simply do not know for sure. And that doesn't frighten me. Quite the opposite. It delights me.

I don't cower in the face of infinite mystery; instead, I pray. I also bake bread. Prayer, baking bread, and baking bread as prayer are the ways I reach toward the infinite mysteries of life and the ways I keep from falling into an apathetic abyss.

I think of baking bread in the same way I think of liturgy—those set prayers, found in the Book of Common Prayer, that I say most days of the month with members of my church community. Some recipes and some prayers are elaborate and involve many ingredients or steps or even special equipment to get it right. Some recipes and prayers are straightforward and so simple, the bread, or the petition, practically bakes (or prays) itself. Some methods are so reliable that the baker gets nearly the same results every time.

Some are not worth the work for the majority of bakers, requiring expensive equipment such as a steam injection oven or terra-cotta cloches hand-forged in France.

To bake bread is to enter into a relationship with your ingredients and also the space in which you are baking. Air temperature and humidity make a difference. The quality of the flour makes a difference. Stone-milled flour tends to be thirstier. The baker who pays attention won't simply measure out to the gram the amount of water indicated in a recipe but will add water or use less initially depending on how wet or dry the dough seems. Or she will add gram for gram the ingredients because that's what the recipe says and most likely will still end up with a pretty good loaf of bread, whether or not she noticed it seemed too dry or too wet.

Years ago, I had a quote from Buddhist monk Thich Nhat Hahn pinned to my bulletin board at work. I've since moved on from that job and in doing so, lost the paper I'd scrawled the words on, and I have not been able to find the quote anywhere so as to get it right, despite all my Google searches and flipping through a couple of books of the monk's. And so, my attributing it to Thich Nhat Hahn could be in error. Still, I return to this wisdom daily and will share it anyway: "What you do does not matter, and yet it is essential that you do it anyway."

That's a hard concept to swallow: that what we do doesn't matter. Especially, if we apply it to prayer. And yet, it can release us from the burden of having to pray "right," to say the right words or ask for the right things. I once led a conversation on prayer with earnest young adults who were at pains to say that prayer shouldn't be about asking for things. "Why not?" I asked them. "It should be about accepting what God has given us," they responded. They were so wary of prayers with an outcome in mind that, I learned, they were avoiding them altogether. As good as their intentions may have been, these young adults had fallen into the trap of "right thinking" when it comes to prayer. Guided by a capital S should and opposed to asking for a specific outcome, they were in fact asking for a specific outcome. Why not just tell God what you're thinking and what you need and want right now? There is no harm in that. My tradition acknowledges personal needs and includes in its prayer book written prayers for everything under the sun: from quiet confidence and guidance in general to guidance in times of conflict and the good use of leisure time. They are great prayers and give words to otherwise quiet but longing hearts.

What's important is to know that what we ask for in our prayer isn't the point of prayer. The point is to acknowledge Infinite Mystery and ourselves. The point of praying is that we pray. In prayer, we put ourselves on holy ground. Because what is prayer other than a means to communicate with God, to transcend ourselves? Praying is the essential thing.

Prayer is a good analogy for baking bread. Baking may not deliver to your hands and mouth exactly what you want, but the baking itself is worth something. You may set out to turn out golden French baguettes worthy of a renowned

Parisian café and end up with something more suitable for slicing thinly into small toasts worthy of a slice of avocado. It is a good thing to show up with an intention, but in the baking something happens that is both worthwhile and mysterious, related to but excessive of what you've come to the baking yearning for.

PAN A L'ANCIENNE

Adapted from *The Bread Baker's Apprentice* by Peter Reinhart

Makes 6 baguettes

This recipe is for a versatile dough that can be shaped into slippers of ciabatta or long, crusty baguettes. It also makes fantastic pizza crust and can be baked in a pan and sprinkled with rosemary and salt for focaccia. It is a wet dough that depends on a long, cold rise in the refrigerator for flavor.

No matter how you bake it, you'll want to return to it regularly to see what else you can

do with it. As Peter Reinhart writes, "This is an exciting place to find oneself, like standing at the end of the world, facing the words that so often showed up on ancient maps, 'Unknown Kingdoms Be Here.'"

---

6 cups (766 g) unbleached bread flour

2¼ teaspoons (16 g) salt

1¾ teaspoons (5 g) instant yeast

2½ cups plus 3 tablespoons (610 g) cool water

flour, semolina, or cornmeal for dusting

---

1. In a large mixing bowl combine flour salt, yeast, and water. Mix with an electric mixer fitted with a paddle attachment on low speed or by hand until a dough comes together, about 1 minute. Continue mixing until the dough pulls away from the sides of the bowl. Transfer to a lightly oiled work surface.

2. Using oiled hands, pat the dough into a disk. Choose one side and stretch it and fold it back in on the dough. Give it a quarter turn and repeat with another side. Repeat two more times for a total of four times. Cover the dough with a bowl and rest for five minutes. Repeat the process, stretching and folding four times, every 5 minutes, four times total. Spray the bowl you've been using to cover the dough lightly with oil. Place the dough in the bowl, turn to coat, and cover. Refrigerate overnight.

3. Bring the dough to room temperature. Gently transfer to a floured work surface using an oiled dough scraper. If the dough is too sticky to handle, lightly sprinkle flour over it. With oiled hands coax it into a roughly 8-inch by 6-inch shape. Divide it cleanly in half, and let it rest for 5 minutes.

4. While from here you can choose your own adventure (see the note above), the directions that follow are for making baguettes.

Arrange an oven rack in the lowest position. Place a metal baking pan in the bottom of the oven. It should be deep enough to hold a cup of water that you'll pour in before baking to provide a steamy environment. Preheat the oven to 500°F or 550°F if it will go that high.

5. Turn two baking sheets upside down and over with parchment. Mist with oil and dust with bread flour, semolina, or cornmeal. With each piece of your divided dough, cut three long portions and transfer to the baking sheets. Using a sharp serrated knife (dip it in water between each cut), score the bread making diagonal slashes across the baguettes.

6. Prepare 1 cup of hot water. Carefully slide one of the pieces of parchment with three of the baguettes onto the baking sheet. Quickly add the water to the bottom of the pan (use an oven mitt because the water will turn to steam when it hits the hot pan) and close the oven door.

7. Bake until golden brown, 20 to 35 minutes, rotating halfway through. Transfer to a cooling rack and repeat the process with the remaining loaves.

FAITH AND DOUBT

WE WERE CAMPING THE FIRST TIME my kid discovered that the flavor pairing of sweet with salty could transcend the sum of its parts. The four-year-old genius (in his mother's eyes anyway) sandwiched a fire-roasted marshmallow between two crisp barbecue chips. A full box of graham crackers sat open on the picnic table alongside the bag of marshmallows and squares of milk chocolate. His eyeballs had just settled on the open bag of chips while he held a stick over the fire to caramelize the exterior of an extra puffy marshmallow. I could see the flash of inspiration in his eyes and wondered what might come of it. Now, whenever we roast marshmallows, someone goes looking for a bag of potato chips.

THE SACRED LIFE OF BREAD

My son has made my heart swell with pride in so many ways in his young life but never so much as when he reveals the culinary adventures he's willing to go on with me. It makes me excited for the journeys we'll take as his palette continues to expand. He is a lover of all kinds of bread and has never once asked me to cut off the crusts. Whether dark rye or the tangiest of sourdough, he loves good bread. If I've got a loaf cooling, he likes that first slice, the one with the crusty end. Yes, I'm bragging, but I know that it was luck of the draw, not some accomplishment on my part that he's willing to eat bread like this.

He has created his own "recipe" already, a way to eat toast that has become a beloved breakfast in our home. Bread, preferably something full flavored and hearty like sourdough, is smeared with a thick layer of butter, drizzled with honey, and sprinkled with wispy flakes of Maldon sea salt. We call it "Albie-style toast."

I was much older than four when I began to discover and understand that the flavors of our favorite foods blossom when paired with their foil. Think salted caramel, trendy for a reason. The flakes of salt tone down the sweetness while also enhancing it, in a mysterious alchemy of flavor. That's what is going on in the Albie-style toast. Cinnamon toast, too, is transformed by a sprinkle of salt. But even before that seasoning gets thrown into the mix, pungent cinnamon is balanced by granulated sugar. The spicy notes are at once enhanced and subdued by the sweetness of the sugar. Sprinkled on buttered toast with a restrained pinch of salt, and a hurried breakfast is something to savor, bite by bite. The butter's richness gives way to the heat of cinnamon, which is balanced by not only the sugar but also the caramelization that has occurred in the toasting of the bread. There is crunch and there is chew, and then the salt heightens the whole experience, enhancing it in an almost revelatory way: It is just cinnamon toast, but it is somehow more than cinnamon toast. More than mere calories shoveled in on the way out the door, it is nourishment at a spiritual level.

That blossoming happens when the flavors hang in the balance. Professional chefs make careers that depend on their ability to create that balance. In *The Flavor Bible*, Karen Page and Andrew Dornenburg say that balance is not simply taste but also mouthfeel and aroma. The crunch of a slice of bread's caramelized exterior is just as important as the chewy interior. And then there is "the X factor," which Page and Dornenburg describe as "what is perceived by the other senses—plus the heart, mind, and spirit." Taste is the perception of the taste buds, mouthfeel by the rest of the mouth, and aroma by the nose. The X factor is that certain something that you can't always put your finger on. Perhaps it is a memory touched by the perceptions of the mouth, taste buds, and nose. Or it could be something else: the way a dish mysteriously suggests a summer breeze off the water or a cozy fire during a bitter storm. Combined, these perceptions become *flavor*, the language of food.

I like this breakdown of flavor. It helps me understand why whenever I'm sad or stressed, I am soothed by a grilled cheese sandwich dipped in, hear me out, tomato ketchup. I'm soothed not only because this is a pairing leftover from childhood but also because beyond the comfort of memory is the present-day pleasure of texture and taste. The combination of crunch from the grilled bread and the salty, unctuous cheese against the sweet tang of ketchup never fails to lighten my occasionally dark spirit and quiet my anxious heart.

There is something in the way that flavor is both the sum of many parts and somehow more than those parts that makes eating a religious experience, a way to encounter God. It affirms my experience that faith is not an intellectual exercise but a multifaceted, multisensory way to live in this world. Spiritual faith, while at once grounded in the experience of being in this world, is likewise the perpetual movement toward transcendence of ourselves, a yearning toward an eternally receding horizon, to use the language of German theologian Karl Rahner. Paradoxically, the more *in* the world we live, the more we can find ourselves moving *beyond* ourselves. A bite of cinnamon toast for breakfast is at once mundane and sacred.

No, faith is not an intellectual exercise. Though our intellect and ability to reason cannot be ignored. There's more to it than belief, but even belief is more than just assenting to a set of statements about one thing or other. *Credo*, the Latin word for "I believe," is different from "I think," *cogito*. I find belief to be more like the X factor of flavor, a perception of more than just the head but also the experience of body and spirit.

Years ago when I was learning how to cook, I went to a cooking demonstration given by Chef Rick Bayless. I don't remember what he made for the group gathered under a small tent at the farmers market, but he said something that has stuck with me and affected my cooking ever since. Home cooks tend to make two mistakes in their kitchens: they don't cook with enough heat and they don't season their food with enough salt. Most home cooks tend to fear using high heat because of the possibility of burning dinner. They under season for fear of making food so salty it becomes inedible. The result is bland, mushy dinners. And here we are again with another insight into the experience of faith brought to us by food. Proverbial heat and salt put to the test and sharpen what we think we know about the world, ourselves, and God. Faith lived in avoidance of trials by fire, of pain and loss, is not faith at all but self-preservation. Faith that avoids experiences and ideas that challenge it is not belief but a rigid way of thinking.

I'm not a proponent of trials by fire. And yet, to go through them can deepen and improve faith like actual fire to actual flavor. Think of that golden crust of a loaf of bread, the part most exposed to the heat of the oven. That exposure means there is a risk of burning. But when you don't cook with enough heat, food is likely to be mushy and flavorless, something like a gently steamed chicken breast with no salt. Bread without a golden crust. Yes, it will sustain you, but it is miserable to eat it. By contrast, recall that until about ten years ago, Brussels sprouts were synonymous with food we hated as children.

Now, everyone loves Brussels sprouts. Nearly one in three restaurants offers some version of them, always pan-roasted because cooking them with high heat makes them deliciously irresistible (especially with crisp bites of salty bacon and a sweet and acidic balsamic vinegar glaze).

Salt is equally if not more important to the flavor of food. In bread baking it does double duty, improving flavor and preventing dough from overproofing. It slows the activity of the yeast and keeps them from petering out. Without salt, bread literally falls flat in flavor and texture. Salt is a lot like doubt when it comes to faith. Rather than faith's opposite, doubt is crucial to full and flourishing faith. In food I think salt is the most important of the tastes, and doubt the most important component of faith.

The people whose faith I admire most tend to be the ones who've experienced a good amount of proverbial salt and heat in their lives. Compared to those who've never endured significant loss or pain, they're the ones most likely to show up when you've endured a life-changing loss.

Not satisfied to leave a tray of lasagna at your doorstop, safely keeping their distance, they will let themselves into your house to take out the garbage and wipe down your counters, despite all your protests that you're *just fine*.

Their own losses and trials having enhanced their faith, they know that if they can help you through this fire of your own, you will emerge golden, good and crusty, and full of flavor, able to show up for others. The most faithful people in my life know deeply that God is most present where two or three are gathered. And so they show up again and again.

In the gospels, there is a story about one of Jesus's followers, a man named Thomas, who became famous for his doubt, so much so that whenever he is mentioned, his name is preceded by this feature of his faith. It was "Doubting Thomas" who had to reach out to touch the body of Jesus after he'd risen from the dead. Doubting Thomas had to put his fingers into the wounds of Jesus's sides to know that not only had he really risen but also he had truly died.

THE SACRED LIFE OF BREAD

I've always had a particular fondness for Thomas. He's someone with whom anyone with a skeptic's mind but a believer's heart can identify with. In the passage of scripture where we get the story of "Doubting Thomas," he's said to not have been with the "other disciples" when they all see Jesus on the road. No one knows why he's not there in the story. Scripture doesn't say. A friend once speculated to me once that maybe he was just running late. I wonder if he was so disappointed with the death of the man he was so convinced would save the world that he called him God, that he needed some time to process and grieve. He'd done everything right, after all: left his former life behind to take up and follow Jesus with a ragtag group of those with the sort of imagination to envision a different kind of world, one in which the poor were rewarded and the rich sent away empty (because, let's face it, they already had enough).

Watching the leader of a movement fueled by hopes and dreams die on a cross, mocked by thug-like soldiers who played a game at the feet of the dying Jesus, his garments going to whoever won, must have wrecked Thomas. And when the other disciples told him that they had seen Jesus, how could Thomas possibly believe it was anything but a cruel joke?

The real mystery in this story to me is that after all that he'd been through, Thomas showed back up at all to be with the disciples for dinner the night that Jesus arrives and Thomas asks to put his hands in the wounds. Thomas rejoins the fellow disciples for a meal, to break bread. He goes back to them, even though all signs pointed to the failure of this mission they thought they were on to bring about a change for the better in the world. All signs said, Go back to your life the way it was before, because all that you'd hoped and dreamed for has come crashing down thanks to the crucifixion.

I think he should be called Faithful Thomas because he showed up, salty as he must have been. Sad as he must have been. I find myself imagining what his faith life was like after that encounter—more two-toned, perhaps richer than that of some of his friends, partaking as it did of both the salty and the sweet.

TOAST, ALBIE-STYLE

1 slice bread
butter
honey
Maldon sea salt

Place a piece of bread, preferably something crusty and full flavored like sourdough, in the toaster. Once toasted, slather with plenty of butter, so that it might dribble onto your chin when you bite into it. Drizzle good honey over the entire slice and finish with a sprinkle of Maldon sea salt.

Variations

1. Use smoked Maldon sea salt instead of plain.

2. Add a pinch of crushed red pepper flakes. Experiment with different kinds such as Aleppo, chipotle, or gochugaru (Korean red pepper flakes).

3. Add a quick grind of black pepper.

IN PLACE

New England hot dog buns are the superior hot dog bun. Flat on either side, they can—and must—be swiped with softened butter and either toasted in a hot pan or thrown on a grill. The result is a buttery, crisp bite into a soft roll that perfectly jackets a salty, snappy hot dog or else sweet chunks of cold lobster bathed in butter or lightly dressed in mayonnaise (I'll allow for both) or crispy fried clams. Really, any food is improved tucked into a properly prepared New England hot dog bun: tuna salad, peanut butter (especially with a crisp slice of bacon), bits of last night's leftovers all get an instant upgrade.

I had never known any other kind of hot dog bun until my family moved from New Hampshire to California the summer before fifth grade. We'd traversed the entire country by car, making extended stops in Hershey, Pennsylvania, to see chocolate get made, St. Louis for a baseball game, and the Petrified Forest before we finally crossed the Colorado River into California and made our way up the long, long, long state into the Sacramento area. I was most captivated by southwestern states; the copper and purple brush strokes across the desert transported me to another world entirely. The food and people of Albuquerque radiated warmth that had a spiritual effect. The whole weeks-long adventure opened my eyes to the boundless array of landscapes, cuisines, and culture.

However, my stepfather, a new addition to our previously girls-only club of my mother, sister, and me, was the only one of us who did not experience a devastating bout of culture shock upon discovering that the rest of the country ate inferior buns with their hot dogs. Rounded with flimsy sides unfit for griddling with butter, they were meant to be eaten straight out of the bag.

Never had I eaten a cold hot dog roll. Microwaving did little good. In fact, it only made things worse. Unevenly and overheated, the rolls became chewy, dense, and dry—the opposite of everything bread should be.

A long-distance phone call was made, and within a few days, a large box, the size one might've found a Commodore 64 home computer in (it was the early 1990s, after all), arrived on the doorstep of our new ranch-style home. The return address said Melrose, Massachusetts. My grandmother had packed the box with at least a half dozen bags of New England hot dog buns—more than seventy buns to last us a few months—as well as several jars of Howard's sweet pepper relish, the sticky, sweet and sour condiment preferred by my family for hot dogs. (Admittedly, I was and remain on the fence about this preference.) Flung three thousand miles from the place my mother, sister, and I knew as *home*, those buns, even that relish, were a lifeline.

The story of this inimitable bun is that Howard Johnson's, the Massachusetts-based restaurant and motel chain, approached a bakery in Maine in the 1940s with an assignment: a roll that would stand upright for filling with fried clams. Slicing a bun on top would allow for the mechanized production of such rolls as well as make it easier to fill with fried clams, serve, and, of course, eat. Although, I've never found a clam roll worth eating easy to eat. The worthiest of clam rolls is the one in which you must go digging through a heaping pile of crispy morsels of the sea to uncover the bun.

I love the New England hot dog bun's origin story because, like so many food traditions, it tells a story about a place. Fried clams are ubiquitous along the New England seacoast. They're inexpensive (or were in my childhood) and fried because not only does dunking them in a hot vat of oil make them delicious, it also increases the amount of time they can be out of the brackish water before going bad. Of course, if you throw them between bread, you've got a meal you can sell and serve to vacationers. Can't you just see white-aproned waiters slinging armloads of clam rolls to families with freckled noses and sunburned shoulders, the good memories of summers spent on the Atlantic Ocean etched into their minds with each bite into those buttery rolls? Who wouldn't want to vacation on the New England coast? Have you ever seen a Winslow Homer painting? The rocky shoreline is even better in person, under the hot summer sun.

That these buns are identified as hot dog buns and not fried clam buns is another new detail in their story that points to place, in this case not just a region but the country. Hot dogs are sausages that likely arrived in the United States with German immigrants in nineteenth century. It is thanks to the bun in which they could be sold at public events—such as baseball games, a beloved source of entertainment in the early twentieth century—that their popularity exploded. They were cheap for sellers, cheap to buyers, easy to handle, and, of course, delicious to eat. In *Hot Dog: A Global History*, Bruce Kraig writes, "Heavy immigration from Europe, the rise of truly large urban centers, new mass entertainments, enhanced information technologies all combined to create a much-desired new national identity, the legendary 'American melting pot.'" Enter the sausage-plus-bun combo, an unintended homage to a place that became synonymous with it, so much so that it is required eating on Independence Day. And although no one seems to remember to actually acknowledge the bun when talking about hot dogs, every illustration, photo, or graphic makes it clear that they're inseparable. Frankly (pun intended), New Englanders just had the right idea for what kind of bun to tuck their dogs into.

Place and identity, whether national, familial, or personal, are connected because, as people, we are embodied, made of stuff, sinew, bones, and blood, and all that stuff needs a place to be. Landscapes, whether rainforest or seacoast, affect how we are, and therefore shape *who* we are. But place is more than land. It is also the communities that inhabit land, the people whose identity is shaped by place and who shape it in return. Identity is both where and how we uncover our lives' meaning. Knowing where we come from can tell us why we are who we are now and can offer hints about where we going.

People claim to hate identity politics, but is there any other kind? Politics is about people, and people crave meaning. The problem is when we become so attached to an identity that we fail to see that all identities have blurry edges. Too often, it's religious identity that is to blame for the borders we create in our lives, whether political or spiritual, an irony especially for Christians, who like to say that an event described in the biblical book of Acts, Pentecost, was the church's birthday. "Now there were devout Jews from every people under heaven living in Jerusalem," writes the author of Acts. As with many gatherings and festivals, the original reason for their togetherness had to do with the harvest. In this case, Jews from all over had gathered to offer thanks to God for the first fruits of the wheat harvest. Well, the Holy Spirit, sent by God soon following the return of the risen Christ to heaven, started blowing through, and suddenly they could all understand each other even though they spoke in the languages of the places from which they'd hailed. A people of distinct identities—expressed in language but certainly also in custom, clothing, and practice—could not deny the existence of one another or claim that their identity should supersede all others' because, thanks to the presence of God so near that it burned, they could understand each other.

The Pentecost story does not speak of a melting pot or even a forging of a new identity for a group. Rather, it acknowledges that we are people of places—and the gift of the story is that place-specific artifacts (specifically language) are not erased for the sake of unity but are transformed from barrier to intelligible gift. Culinary preferences, even preferences for hot dog buns, can be the same—markers of place-moored identity that can be more gift than barrier. That said, even if I commit myself to finding others' culinary preferences intelligible, I'm not willing to give up my hot dog bun evangelism just yet. *Evangel* means *good news*, after all, and there

are plenty who have yet to hear and experience
the wonder of the straight-sided roll.

Supposedly there is a market for New England
hot dog buns in Florida, home to retired snow-
birds who make their way south for the winter.
Despite my efforts, there is not yet a market in
Chicago. The buns are available on the world's
largest online retailer, but at $20.99 for a dozen,
I'd rather eat a mediocre bun, or better yet, no
bun at all. Chicago has its own style of hot dog
bun, and I have tried to get used to it, although
after twenty years, I still find the soft, steam-
warmed poppy seed rolls disappointing. They are
merely a vehicle for transporting an otherwise
transcendent assortment of pickle, relish, diced
onion, mustard, sliced tomato, and celery salt
atop a snappy hot dog to your mouth.

I've taken matters into my own hands and
have started making my own New England hot
dog buns. It is a bittersweet endeavor, as I move

through the memories associated with my child-hood. When I portion out the ten pieces of dough and roll them into balls, I think of my family, scattered across space and time. My grandmother who diligently packed and sent rolls and relish has now passed away, as have my beloved aunt and godmother whose pool we sat by through the years eating hot dogs topped with Howard's sweet pepper relish. My family never returned to New England to live; my sister and mother (since divorced from my stepfather) are in Virginia. My cousins are scattered across New England and have laid roots in new places, with new communities of friends and family.

When I roll the buns into ovals, the next step in shaping them, I experience a strange spiritual longing for my scattered memories, mostly symbols, sounds, and smells now, the details having evaporated like mist over the ocean on a rapidly warming summer morning. Now it's all just salty air, sunshine, and a sense of security and love for the people who were always counting the ways we knew we belonged to each other: freckles, blue eyes, ferocious appetites.

IN PLACE

Rolling my palm across each oval so they become cylindrical and arranging them in the specially designed pan for baking hot dog rolls, I recall my cousins squeezing shoulder to shoulder so one of the aunts or uncles could take a picture. I picture us huddled together on Christmas Eve, singing carols for the neighbors from our grandparents' porch.

Almost as soon as they've been baked and are cool enough to handle, a single roll gets torn into three portions, and I'm firmly situated in my kitchen handing out pieces like communion bread to my family. My husband gets it now and, if given a choice, will opt for the superior bun, though it's not as if there's ever an option for anything else in our home—lucky he has me to keep them in supply. My son gets it too, and I watch his eyes roll back in ecstasy every time he bites into the rolls. My own eyes get misty whenever this happens. I know I'm handing him not just a piece of bread but a piece of myself.

NEW ENGLAND HOT DOG ROLLS

Adapted from *Also the Crumbs Please*

I stumbled on this recipe from a UK-based, Austrian food blogger after several failed attempts at my favorite rolls using recipes from much more well-known sources. I'll never tell who, but I did purchase a special pan from one whose name references an English monarch of legend.

The pan is not strictly necessary, but it is recommended and can be purchased online. If you don't have one, line the rolls up on a parchment-lined baking sheet side by side so

they're touching. The outermost rolls won't
have the flat edge, but the rest will.

---

3 cups (375 g) bread flour

¼ cup (28 g) nonfat dry milk

2 tablespoons (11 g) instant potato flakes

2 tablespoons (25 g) sugar

1¼ teaspoons (8 g) salt

1¾ teaspoons (7 g) instant yeast

2 large eggs, plus 1 more for an egg wash

½ cup (120 g) water

¼ cup (60 g) full-fat milk

5 tablespoons (71 g) unsalted butter, at
room temperature

---

1. In a large bowl, add the flour, dry milk,
   potato flakes, sugar, salt, yeast, 2 eggs, water,
   and milk and knead either by hand or on
   low speed in a stand mixer fitted with the
   hook attachment until the dough comes

together, about 3 to 4 minutes in the mixer or 5 to 6 minutes by hand, scraping down the sides of the bowl halfway through. Once it comes together, let it rest for 30 minutes.

2. After resting, knead the dough (on low speed in a mixer) and gradually add the butter until it is completely incorporated. Once all of the butter is incorporated, knead until the dough is smooth and releases from the sides of the bowl, 4 to 6 minutes on high speed in a mixer, 5 to 7 minutes by hand. It should be very soft and satiny and slightly tacky to the touch.

3. Transfer the dough to a lightly oiled bowl and turn to coat. Cover and allow to rise until doubled in size, about 2 hours. (At this point, if you wish to bake the following day, rest the dough at room temperature until it has grown slightly. Then put it in the refrigerator and let rest overnight. The next day, allow dough to come to room temperature before moving on.)

4. Tip the dough, gently coaxing it out of the bowl and onto a lightly oiled work surface. Divide into 10 equal pieces. With lightly oiled fingers, roll each bowl into a ball and press into a disk. Then stretch and fold each side, 6 to 8 times, into the center to form a tight ball with smooth tension on the top and the seams on the bottom. Then place the ball seam-side down and gently roll in a circular motion on the work surface with your hand in a C-shape. The seams should close up on the bottom. Repeat for each piece of dough. Then gently roll each piece back and forth under your palm to create an oval. Cover with a piece of plastic wrap lightly sprayed with oil and allow to rest for 10 minutes.

5. Lightly spray a hot dog pan if using. Roll each piece of dough into a 5-inch cylinder and place into the pan or onto a parchment-lined baking sheet. Cover again and rest at room temperature until doubled in size, about 45 minutes to 1 hour.

6. Preheat the oven to 400°F 20 minutes before ready to bake. Whisk an egg with a few drops of water to make an egg wash and brush the tops of the buns. Bake until golden brown, 18 to 20 minutes.

7. When the rolls come out of the oven, leave them in the pan and brush with melted butter and cover with a clean, dry tea towel for 20 minutes. Then uncover, remove from the pan and cool completely on a rack. They will still be in one large piece. Separate into individual rolls and split by cutting in the center of each roll, without cutting all the way through. (I leave them together and refrain from splitting until ready to serve in order to prevent them from drying out.)

8. You know what to do next: swipe with softened butter and grill in a hot pan just before filling with hot dogs, fried clams, or whatever your heart desires.

SOURDOUGH

IF YOU HAVE NO SPIRITUAL PRACTICES in your life or are looking for a new spiritually edifying habit to maintain, may I suggest a sourdough starter? Part science experiment, part culinary adventure, caring for one is so much simpler than anyone ever makes it out to be. Yes, a starter calls for discipline, but it is forgiving. When I can no longer sustain a regular baking practice, either because of the demands of parenthood or my job or I am avoiding cranking the oven up in the summer, I will tuck my starter in for a long, cold nap in the back of the fridge. The yeast will go dormant, sluggishly eating and releasing gas and alcohol, but it is not likely to die.

THE SACRED LIFE OF BREAD

A sourdough starter can go dormant for ages and still have enough life in it that reviving it takes only a week or so of feedings. When the time is right, you can return to it again. A little attention and care and it goes from merely alive to vigorous and flourishing mere days, just waiting to transform the most mundane of dough into sublime bread. Tell me there's not a spiritual lesson in that. Just because we set down spiritual practices does not mean we will not or cannot return to them.

One of my favorite words is *yet*. I also like the phrase *right now*. I am not in the regular practice of baking sourdough weekly *right now*; it is too hot outside, and my oven should not be in a battle with my air conditioner lest I want to wear them both out. I'm not tending to the starter in the back of my refrigerator *right now* because it is December, and I would rather spend my free time celebrating the season with friends and family. I haven't revived the sourdough *yet* because I know that the demands of my personal life would only frustrate my ability to show up regularly.

SOURDOUGH

Spiritual practices can come and go, depending on your life's circumstances. They can go dormant but not die. Maybe you used to wake every morning to write, pray, or do yoga, but you had kids who wake up just as early as you—or earlier. Maybe you just wanted more sleep. Or maybe you were recovering from a back injury and had to refrain from yoga on a doctor's orders. Your practice isn't lost or dead. You're just not doing it *right now*. I used to ride my bike twenty-two miles round trip to work three or four days a week. It was my spiritual as well as physical exercise. Cruising alongside sparkling Lake Michigan, wind in my hair, this was my morning and evening prayer. It's been ten years since I had this practice. I am not likely ever to fully return to it, but I haven't given up. Just as I might revive my starter for only a loaf or two, I cycle along the lakefront whenever the time is right.

You can feed a starter with all sorts of things. Some people toss in unpeeled fruits, such as grapes or peaches, claiming the wild yeasts that cling to the fruits' skins improve the starter's flavor or turn up the fermentation to Level Extremely Vigorous. Some swear by pineapple juice for its sugars and acidity. That's all well and good, but all you really need is flour and water and time. A pinch of commercial yeast can help get things going if you're not feeling confident.

One of the hardest things about maintaining a sourdough starter is how much gets discarded each week or every few days depending on how often you're baking. Week after week, you add fresh water and fresh flour but only after tossing half of what is already there. I've tried to avoid the discard, thinking I'd use extra starter for crackers, pancakes, muffins. But it gets unwieldy fast. With each feeding, the starter exponentially increases in size and volume.

I once interviewed a professional baker who told me that he would thinly spread discarded starter over an oiled silicone baking mat, then coat it with sesame, pumpkin, and poppy seeds and bake it until crisp. Finally, he'd drizzle it with honey fresh out of the oven. I tried this method once, and broken into large shards, the baked starter is a perfect cracker-like accompaniment to a cheese board, dipped in hummus, or eaten straight away before it's even had a chance to cool.

Creative uses for discarded starter aside, having to reduce the starter by half with each feeding is another opportunity for spiritual growth. Discarding starter can help cultivate the ability to let go and hold lightly to what we have today. If you're anything like me, that's an important lesson. If one of Mary's monikers were Our Lady of Perpetual Worry, I would be her most pious devotee. My anxiety about What Might Happen and how I can prevent or be prepared for it is always simmering just beneath the surface of my thoughts. I especially hate to throw away food out of an acknowledgment that it may not always be so readily and abundantly available. My secret superpower is my ability to turn bits and bobs of leftovers and about-to-expire pantry items into delicious meals, a superpower born out of anxiety, no doubt. But maintaining my sourdough starter these past years has been at least as much about holding on to things with a lighter touch as it has been about making delicious bread. Maintaining starter is a regular opportunity to practice letting go of worry about what I might need it for later, and therefore an opportunity to get comfortable with the letting go of all my "what if's." A compost bin helps enormously by helping me to think less about tossing what I could use or might need and more about returning to the soil what once grew there. (I've yet to find a compost bin for all my "what if's.")

There are stories about centuries-old starters. Congratulations to whomever has the confidence to make bold proclamations of provenance and history about something that lives in a refrigerator. I do not. I've been maintaining my starter for only about five years. It started as an all-wheat starter, then became all-rye. Now it's back to all-wheat. It's gone dormant at least six or seven times and sometimes for six months. The only real reason to toss a starter is if it gets pink, which is a sign that the bad bacteria that can make you very sick have taken over. Even mold can be scraped off if the top gets a little fuzzy.

I am especially impressed by stories bakers tell of dehydrating and rehydrating their starters in order to travel with them across the country. I worked with a young woman who took her starter with her for a semester in Florence and later moved with it to Denver from Madison, Wisconsin. She slowly dried it out each time and then just added water when she got to her destination, like you'd do with a pouch of dinner while backpacking. I am moved by bakers who've cared for the starter their grandmothers entrusted to them like heirlooms from the Old Country but have only heard stories secondhand. Admittedly, the idea of an heirloom sourdough starter is quite romantic and so I'd love to enjoy bread with that much history, even if the yeast that gave it its rise were the billionth descendants of the original starter.

It's the science behind these strange, bubbling mixtures of flour, water, and yeast that I find utterly enchanting. Fermentation, the anaerobic (meaning without oxygen, thank you high school biology) process by which nutrients are broken down into energy, is the mystery of life at work in our own kitchens. In this process, strange and wonderful things happen. What is inedible and tasteless becomes extraordinarily delicious. I took a baking class, in which I received my current starter, with cookbook author Peter Reinhart, who remarked that fermentation brings the dead back to life. When wheat berries are milled, either crushed between stones or pressed between rollers, its life-giving properties are destroyed. No longer can it be planted into the soil to become yet another plant producing more seeds. But fermentation resurrects it. A sourdough starter is the breath of life added to unliving clay.

Sandor Katz, the author of *The Art of Fermentation*, goes so far as to say that fermentation plays an important role in the evolution of life, beginning with the emergence of life on this planet. "Fermenting bacteria are thought to have emerged relatively early from the primordial prebiotic soup, before the atmosphere had a sufficient concentration of oxygen to support or evolve aerobic life-forms," he writes. Fermentation changed everything.

In his thick volume of collected research on the history and methods for krauts, kravasses, beers, kimchis, and other fermented foods from around the globe, Katz writes that much of the food and drink we love to eat and imbibe—beer, cheese, bread, sake, cured meats, and yogurt— are thanks to fermentation. The discovery that we could extend the life of edible plants and proteins had a considerable impact on our human lives. The ability to preserve food through fermentation allowed us to evolve, to live better outcomes such as longevity. But the preservation of food does not only translate to the preservation of life. It also improves food and therefore life.

Consider grapes. For one, they're not easy to grow. My husband and I once rented the first-floor apartment of a two-flat that came with a postage-stamp garden where two grape vines wrapped merrily around the border in parallel lines. The owners had given up on the vines after years and years of cultivation and told me I could have the garden to myself. Come summer, the vines produced small, shriveled green grapes that were incredibly sour. I know nothing about cultivating grapes and decided to just let the grapes be decorative. My appreciation for the generations of vineyard tenders, however, grew.

Grapes are highly perishable. Out of the refrigerator and left on the counter, it's only a matter of hours before the fruit flies appear for a feast of sweet, rotting fruit. If you press the grapes to extract their juices, you can refrigerate the juice (but for no more than a week) or pasteurize it under high temperatures to kill off potentially harmful bacteria, as most processors do before sealing and selling it in square and squeezable boxes. Or you can ferment it.

But once fermented, that juice is no longer just juice. It is transformed into wine. Fruit of the vine, the work of human hands. A spiritual drink. We call the best of this transformed liquid "fine." As Katz puts it, that wine is not simply a "stable, coveted commodity" thanks to fermentation but something of an elixir. It tastes of the soil in which the grapes grew, the terroir. It smells of other fruits—berries and cherries—and savors of dark chocolate or leather. If you can smell underripe stone fruit or imagine a bushel of tart green apples, it's thanks to fermentation.

If you sip a glass of wine and taste bright blades of grass or inhale sunshine and lemons, say thank you to the tiny organisms that have taken up residence on the skins of grapes or tucked themselves cozily into the wood of aging barrels. Fermentation improves food. It improves life. And like with bread, the more wine you make, the better the wine gets, not just because of the accumulation of wisdom, though that's certainly part of it, but the conditions that allow for robust fermentation only improve the more fermentation that occurs. Spend four weeks baking a loaf or two a week, and you'll know what I mean. The bread just rises with more ease. The baker relaxes too in her newfound and growing wisdom.

Several years before the pandemic, my husband decided he was tired of paying nearly four dollars for a bottle of kombucha. "It's more expensive than beer!" he'd say when I'd pick up a bottle of GT's guava-flavored brew. So he decided to start making it at home. Turns out you can make gallons of the stuff for pennies at home as long as you have a scoby—an acronym for symbiotic culture of bacteria and yeast and resembles a sort of tentacle-less jellyfish that looks as if it belongs in the deepest trenches of the ocean, nestled among the deep-sea hydrothermal plumes with all the other bacteria. But lay this strange and layered blob on top of freshly brewed sweet tea, and two weeks later, you have kombucha, made at a fraction of the cost. After success with homebrewed kombucha, my husband looked at another expensive habit of ours: premium organic yogurt. Since then, he's spoiled our family with freshly made yogurt at least once, often twice, a week. The benefits have not only been financial. My bread dough now becomes pillowy with little effort. There is something of a "passing on" that has happened thanks to the cultures he uses in our kombucha and yogurt. He's created a thriving environment for fermentation to occur. And these staples of tea, yogurt, and flour benefit from that.

Katz points out that we use the word *culture* to refer to the element meant to initiate fermentation, often called a starter or a mother, such as with vinegar: "Simultaneously, culture constitutes the totality of all that humans seek to pass from generation to generation, including language, music, art, literature, scientific knowledge, and belief systems, as well as agriculture and culinary techniques (in both of which fermentation occupies a central role)." Culture is the stuff that makes life worth living that we want to pass on and share with others.

Although Katz makes only passing references to religion, it is impossible for me to read his reflections on fermentation as a "coevolutionary force" and not think of the incarnation, of the divine made present. In *The Supper of the Lamb*, Episcopal priest Robert Farrar Capon writes that "if we are fascinated, even intoxicated, by matter, it is no surprise: we are made in the image of the Ultimate Materialist." Though wary of drawing neat lines between the description of natural processes that belong in biology texts and any sort of spiritual reflection, I have to marvel in observation and delight at the fact of fermentation, a process with which we living beings interact intimately whether we realize it or not. I am moved on a spiritual level by learning what happens in the matter of this world. Perhaps neat lines need not be drawn. Perhaps one simply overlays the other so that they are indistinguishable. To encounter holiness doesn't require us to transcend our bodies or the stuff of our lives. Our lives are already holy, full of mystery and wonder and surprise. Fermentation is a process that reveals that holiness. Caring for a sourdough starter is an opportunity to know more intimately how sacred the stuff of our lives is, right down to the bacteria and yeast that make ordinary bread extraordinary.

SOURDOUGH

In *The Bread Baker's Apprentice*, Reinhart writes about the baker's "altar of transformation." The book is not a religious text. He means an ordinary baker, not The Baker, as if that were another name for God. This altar is not a specific table or even location such as a breadboard or kitchen countertop where ingredients are combined, kneaded, and shaped. Perhaps that's what he meant to say, but instead, he says that it's just a handful of "essentials" that make an altar of transformation. He likens it to mise en place, a concept known well to bakers, chefs, and even home cooks, that translates from the French to "everything in its place." What it means is that all of the ingredients and tools the chef or baker or home cook will need in order to work their alchemy are available and at hand: ingredients, an oven, bowls, kitchen utensils, and a place to work. A location on which to perform the ritual of baking is part of the altar of transformation.

I find this idea of a baker's altar of transformation, perhaps for obvious reasons, particularly salient. I'm a priest, after all. What we call God's altar is the place where I find myself most reverent and in awe. There, I feel at once myself and also as if I've been plunged into something other worldly. I experience a profound connection to the community I serve, the dinner party that has gathered for this ridiculous meal of bread and wine where the incarnate God becomes fully present. There is a mystical dimension to presiding at an altar, praying, remembering, recalling how the goodness and graciousness of the divine has suffused all things with pure, life-giving presence, even, and especially, in times of sorrow, oppression, and death. My own sense of the transformation that takes place in the prayers and the gathering of people I lead is not that my hands, which I swoop and then hover over a chalice and a moon-shaped wafer of bread, turn these things into the body and blood of Jesus, but that my role is to reveal what is *already there*: the presence of something ineffable and mysterious in simple bread and wine. Bread and wine, already sacred, become mysteriously even more so. Often on Sunday mornings, I think of Jesus upon a mountain with his inner circle, revealing to them who he truly is: at once as human as Adam, made of dust, and as cosmic as stardust. The source of all existence.

I'm sometimes reluctant to admit it—to map any tidy lines from one place to the next—but there is a correlation between what happens when I'm standing at an altar in a church and when I'm hunched over my kitchen counter. Still, the space in which bread becomes bread is its own kind of altar of transformation. The room, the oven, the air, the wild yeasts and microbes, and the baker herself are all essential to the many cycles of transformation that will take place over the long process of turning flour, water, yeast, and salt into a loaf of bread. They create community together, an invitation and an opportunity to settle into themselves, to be who they truly are, in something both mystical and earthy, joyful and substantive.

While his most famous book is not overtly religious, Reinhart *is* religious, in a most generously kind and curious way. He has written a spiritual memoir, *Bread on Water*, in which he reflects on his journey that took him from the Hare Krishnas to an intentional Christian community and eventually to Eastern Orthodoxy and the role of bread in that journey. He braids together the narratives of his own spiritual questing and his evolving life as a baker. But even when writing for an audience that just wants to learn his secrets to good bread, Reinhart can't help but let it slip that a life in pursuance of soft, buttery dinner rolls and hearty loaves of caraway seed–flecked pumpernickel is one of meaning, hope, and, above all, transformation.

I met Reinhart at a bread baking clinic in a far-flung western suburb of Chicago. I took the day off work, drove nearly two hours in rush-hour traffic straight west of the city, and arrived only minutes before the clinic started. The last seat available was front and center. I perched myself on the high stool and looked around at the other attendees, who all seemed to know each other and were chatting with one another. Reinhart began the class by handing out a thick packet of recipes and reflections from his book. I took copious notes as soon as he began to speak.

"Ultimately, bread is a transformational food," he said. He spoke of the transfiguration of tasteless flour into dough and eventually bread that, emerging from the oven, looks nothing like what goes into it. Bread holds a special place in people's hearts and in religious traditions and festivals. That's not a coincidence, he suggested. The baker engages deeply with this transformation process, a process too often confined to the realm of religion and spirituality. But baking bread could be a spiritual practice in and of itself. At the time, I had recently been made a "postulant" in the Episcopal Church, that is, someone publicly discerning a particular ministry as well as undergoing intentional formation for a life in that role. For me that meant anti-racism training, classes on Anglican history and church law, and time spent working at a church as well as a hospital. No one had assigned me to attend a bread clinic as part of my postulant's formation, but my time spent with Reinhart and alongside other bakers turned out to be just as important for my formation as a priest as my several months praying at hospital bedsides.

There is a corollary here between the processes of spiritual transformation and fermentation. Fermentation in bread, whether thanks to commercial yeast or carefully tended to sourdough, is special. It makes the bread possible. Baking sourdough bread continues to be essential for my ongoing spiritual transformation.

Reinhart invited us into the act of transforming "wheat to eat." And we got to work, shaping floppy, wet dough into ciabatta, small, chewy slipper-shaped loaves. (The word *ciabatta* means *slipper* in Italian.) Next, we combined wheat bran, cooked brown rice, and whole wheat flour with milk, butter, and honey to make Struan, an old harvest festival bread whose name refers to the merging of two streams. It's also one of Reinhart's favorite breads, as it is a recipe he developed and wrote about in his first book, *Brother Juniper's Bread Book: Slow Rise as Method and Metaphor*, another of those books in which he can't help but point out that the way bread is made reflects something deeper at the heart of reality and how baking allows us to reach in and touch that mystery, even if the tips of our fingers only just graze it.

Recently, I pulled a dormant sourdough starter from my fridge. The hooch, the alcoholic byproduct that the yeast secretes after eating the sugars in the flour, had turned a murky, seawater gray. I poured off the liquid and stuck my nose into the wide mouth quart jar for a sniff test. The scent of it was a bouquet of charred oak, vanilla, and springtime. A memory was triggered and I was immediately sent on a journey to my favorite neighborhood pub, a Belgian-style bar that serves hot buttery mussels in broth with half baguettes and a piping hot frites, served in a paper cone with miniature cups of thick, garlicky aioli. Things just smell ferment-y there, in the best possible way. Life bubbles away vigorously in this pub, in the beer, in the bread, in the people who gather.

I recalled an afternoon when I left work early for a haircut and then, with freshly trimmed bangs, made my way to this sacred watering hole for a bite and a pint before the after-work crowd filed in. The air would be vibrating with the din of conversation in just a few short hours, but it was quiet for now. A couple in the corner leaned their heads together as they pored over the extensive menu of draft and bottle beers, occasionally coming up for air to take in the vintage signs. My husband and I spent ten childless years seeking out the best and most beloved off-the-beaten-path watering holes when we traveled, and there was a likeness to the couple that I recognized. I guessed that they were not from here but adventurers from another neighborhood, state, or perhaps even country.

I'm not a heavy drinker. I cannot have more than two of anything without suffering the consequences for a full day or two afterward. I love to quaff a crisp lager on the hottest days and sip fine wine while indulging in a good novel. Cocktails made bright with citrus and a salt rim, unmixed spirits poured straight into a glass, dark and brooding. This may scandalize the Methodist teetotalers I know and love, but I believe all these beverages offer a taste of heaven, most especially when quaffed not at home but in a bustling pub. I blame the fermentation that made them possible and also the presence of others, whether squeezed in snug as sardines into a corner booth, with friends perched at a bar top, or alone with my book, imbibing and eating. Breaking bread in the presence of others, being together, sharing stories, surrounded in a cloud of conversation is sacred space. Here is another altar of transformation.

Should it be any wonder that I'm sent to that altar simply by smelling my dormant sourdough starter? Even dormant, it is alive, always beckoning me back to a practice that I love and that changes me, even if I have set it down for a while.

ALMOST WHOLE GRAIN SOURDOUGH BREAD

Makes 1 loaf

My friend Jeffrey, whom I credit with the inspiration for this recipe, boldly makes a 100 percent whole grain sourdough. I get nearly there in my sourdough, and that's good enough for me. He uses a blend of einkorn, black emmer, dark rye, and whole wheat as well as more water to account for the additional bran and germ of the whole grain flours. If you don't have rye and emmer, you can substitute with whole wheat.

A recipe follows for a rye sourdough starter.

1¾ cups (375 g) room temperature water

½ cup plus 1 tablespoon (150 g) starter, 8 to 10 hours after feeding

2 cups (200 g) dark rye

1¼ cups (125 g) black emmer

1½ cups (200 g) high-protein bread flour

2¼ teaspoons (0.5 g) salt

---

1. In a large bowl, combine the water and starter. Using your fingers, gently break up the starter so that it dissolves. Add the flours and stir with a dough whisk, a wooden spoon, or your fingers until it comes together in a shaggy ball of dough. Cover with a damp towel and rest for 30 minutes.

2. Sprinkle half the salt over the top of the dough and press in using damp fingers. Fold the dough over on itself and repeat with the remaining salt until dissolved into the dough. Stretch and fold the top,

the bottom, and then both sides. Allow it to rest for 15 to 30 minutes. Repeat 4 times.

3. After the final fold, rest the dough for 2 hours, which, according to Jeffrey, gets it to smell "barn-like and yogurty." Then cover it and place it in the fridge for 20 hours. It's OK if it sits for longer. Just pull it out within two days when you're ready to bake.

4. Punch down the dough and knead a few times. Allow it to rest for about 30 minutes, then shape as desired. Proof for 2 to 3 hours. About 30 minutes before baking, preheat a Dutch oven in a 500°F oven.

5. Carefully transfer the dough to the preheated Dutch oven and score with a blade or serrated knife. Bake covered at 500°F for 30 minutes. Remove the cover and bake for another 5 minutes or until the crust is well-bronzed and golden.

6. Cool completely before serving.

RYE SOURDOUGH STARTER

That same baker who gave me the great idea for using discarded starter also taught me about maintaining a "micro starter." In this method, you bake once you have enough starter, meaning there is far less to discard. Begin by mixing together 1 cup each of rye and all-purpose flour. You'll use this flour mixture to start and feed your starter in the beginning.

Please note that I tend to ignore every rule out there about dividing and discarding starter. Once I have an active starter going, I begin building it up for baking without discarding and

by adding double the weight of the starter in
flour and water. This works for me. My breads
rise easily and taste great. If it doesn't work for
you, the internet is home to endless guides to
creating a starter "the right way."

---

10 g (1 heaping tablespoon) flour mixture

10 g (2½ teaspoons) lukewarm, filtered
water (chlorine in some municipal water
can kill yeasts)

---

1. In a clean glass jar, vigorously stir together
   the flour and water. Cover and mark the side
   of the jar. Every day, check to see if there is
   activity. Once you notice that it is smelling
   pungent and the top is dotted with bubbles,
   pour off any gray liquid that has collected on
   top (you may not have any of this), and feed
   daily for about a week (4 to 10 days).

2. To feed, divide the starter in half, transferring 10 grams (2 teaspoons) into a new jar. Discard the rest. Add another 10 grams of flour and water each. Stir vigorously and scrape the sides down. Cover.

3. The starter may rise and fall over this period, perking up and settling back down over the course of the day.

4. After about a week, you can begin building up your starter to ready it for baking and storing. You can also switch to all rye flour if desired. Begin by discarding all but 10 grams of starter. Feed it with 10 grams each flour and water. The next day, increase the feeding to 20 grams each without discarding any starter. The following day, as long as the starter is active, increase the feeding to 40 grams each, and so on. If it does not rise and fall over the course of a day, return to 10 grams and start again.

Repeat until you have a little more starter than you need. (Keep some to build up for your next loaf.)

5. Feed your starter 12 hours before baking. It is ready when a tablespoon of it floats in water.

IRISH SODA BREAD

EVERY YEAR ON ST. PATRICK'S DAY, WE would eat Irish Bread, what most people call soda bread. I'm not sure why we didn't call it soda bread. All I know is that "Irish Bread" is what is written on the top of the three-by-five-inch index cards with the recipe that circulates in my family. There are two handwritten versions, one in my preadolescent hand (complete with a bubble over the lowercase *i* in Irish) and one in my grandmother's elegant cursive that swoops and curls in royal blue ink.

It took me a long time to attempt making Irish bread on my own. The first time I made it was in the fall, clear on the other end of the year from St. Patrick's Day. For most of my early adulthood, after succumbing once to drunken revelry on March 17 the first year I lived in Chicago, I came to the conclusion that I was too authentically Irish to celebrate St. Patrick's Day. In a paradoxical feat of mental gymnastics, I opted out of acknowledging the holiday that Irish Americans have long adopted as a celebration of their identity in order to somehow take that part of my identity more seriously. Plus, the few times I'd call my mother to ask for the recipe, I'd be reminded that it calls for raisins. I hate raisins.

My grandmother's recipe is odd, to say the least. It doesn't even call for baking soda. Perhaps this is the reason for its name. It does, however, call for a whopping six teaspoons of baking powder, approximately two tablespoons—mysterious insofar as six teaspoons is a lot of baking powder, but also why not just say what six teaspoons equals: two tablespoons? Baking powder does contain baking soda, as well as cream of tartar and sometimes cornstarch. Was the plain baking soda hard to come by for whomever wrote this recipe? Or was it the buttermilk that was hard to find and they needed to make sure something acidic was included to interact with the baking soda? Cream of tartar, the acidic byproduct of winemaking, would provide that. But the recipe calls for sour cream, which is acidic and richer than buttermilk, as well as milk. The ingredient list is a mystery, the history of which I'll likely never uncover.

My mother insists that if the recipe had been tweaked or changed, it would have had to have been before it was handed on to my grandmother. "Grandma didn't play with recipes or ingredients," my mother told me. "She was too worried about wasting them." A trait, evidently, that was handed down. Some children inherit wealth, others anxiety over lack of it. Whenever I attempted cookies on my own as a preteen, my mother would get exasperated when I, who was convinced I was a kitchen witch, excited to perform the great alchemy of mixing ingredients into something magical, would usually dive into a recipe so hastily I wouldn't even read it but instead take inspiration from it—often leading to inedible results. It was then that my mother would pass on the kitchen wisdom she had received from her mother: Read your recipe at least twice and follow it to a T. Do not try out your ideas. Stick to what is in front of you.

As a kid, I liked the sweet-sour taste of caraway seeds, licorice-like in flavor, gently laced through our family's Irish bread, spread over with a thick layer of margarine (because I grew up in the fat-phobic '80s and '90s). But when I finally baked the original recipe, I was appalled. It calls for so many teaspoons of caraway seeds (six! Again, foregoing a standard measurement, two tablespoons, and way too much) that I could not get the taste of them out of my mouth. It was if I had eaten an entire loaf of deli rye but with none of the accompaniments that make deli rye so delicious (pastrami, smoked salmon, mustard, sauerkraut, pickles). To try to salvage the loaf, I spread not margarine, per my child-hood, but a creamy-tangy layer of cultured butter over a slice—this improved matters considerably. (Spreadable margarine, by the way, offends even more bluntly than stale communion hosts in that it barely hints at the thing to which it points rather than offering a small but full taste of the Real Thing.)

One thing this recipe does get right is that it says to bake in a greased cast-iron "fry pan," which I actually own. The tall sides allow the bread to rise upward in the oven instead of spreading outward. The real reason I delight in this instruction is that I think of my unmarried great-aunts, whose home always smelled of turnips according to my mother, shaping loaves of Irish Bread into pans just like the one I insisted on buying on a road trip stop at a Lodge store outlet. I didn't know why I needed the fry pan then. I rarely deep fry anything. But every time I wrestle it off a high shelf in my kitchen, it is an homage to the wide Irish women I descend from.

This recipe, this bread is as odd and complicated as my relationship to my ancestry. I don't imagine I'm alone in having such a history tied up in a family recipe. When my no-deviations-from-the-recipe Irish Bread is in the oven,

I call my mother to ask her whether she recalled her mother baking this bread when she was young or if it was something her mother decided to reclaim as her heritage later in life, like I have. Oh, yes, she says. And she did not like the bread at all. She was a picky child, and her taste buds could not bear the offense of raisins *plus* caraway seeds. Only as an adult did she start to not only eat it but bake it for her own family every year in honor of her ancestry. She didn't deviate from the recipe, of course. But I think that had as much to do with wanting the way we honored our Irishness to be authentic as much as the anxiety about frugality (though, that anxiety is also in homage to our Irish heritage). If this recipe came from grandma, who got it from her mother, then it was really Irish. Therefore, we were really Irish. And that was important to her. It still is. My mother had her DNA tested to confirm it. She's 100 percent.

In the United States, we are obsessed with authenticity. I witness this especially around St. Patrick's Day. Every year, I read some think piece or Facebook post critiquing so-called Irish Americans for their display of pride. There are those in the staunch, "I'm authentically Irish," camp who snobbishly remind everyone of their own authenticity by bemoaning how Americans taint this "actually important religious holiday." As if dying a river green were an affront to their very sense of selves. No better are those with no claim to Irish identity who delight in their above-it-all perspective, rolling their eyes at anyone who could call themselves Irish after having lived in North America for four generations. "You're just white Americans now," claimed an op-ed I read recently, as if the not quite 200 years spent on this continent cancels out the thousand years lived on another. And finally, there are those with perhaps the fairest critique who rightly wonder why we can't have secular feast days as widely embraced for other non-European immigrant groups.

So often, whenever people are upset about something, the something is not the actual culprit. Rather, a longing or a hurt simmers below the surface, the true source of indignation.

THE SACRED LIFE OF BREAD

Beneath the yearly essays on "authentic" Irish-ness as well as the green-beer-chugging and whiskey-shot-gulping is a longing for identity and truth, a story with beginnings that stretch back more than fifty years. As religious institutions decline and the cult of the individual finds increasingly new ways to be practiced, we have lost ways to connect to something bigger than ourselves. We're not devoid of means of connection; we've only lost some of the ways humans have been making meaning for thousands of years. No matter how much we may want them to, exercise bikes and Instagram are never going to be a sustainable means of intimacy or transcendence.

I, too, wrestle with "authenticity." I wonder if I even ought to refer to myself as Irish. My mother may boast 100 percent Irish ancestry, but mine is more varied. I've never even been to Ireland. The only vestige of my ancestors' home left in me is my pale pink, freckled skin and my name. And even that is perhaps the least Irish part about me. Murphy comes from my father who himself is "less Irish" than his name would suggest. Likewise, I've hyphenated my own name with my husband's English one and I am a priest in a church in the Anglican tradition. What would my great-aunts make of that? And yet, I admittedly ache to sink the bottoms of my feet into the soil across the sea, to smell the air where "my people" baked and broke bread before sailing across the ocean in search of enough to eat.

The name "soda bread" refers directly to one of the rising agents (baking soda) in this humble method of turning inexpensive and available ingredients into what was the only thing on the table during famine years. When combined with the acidity of sour milk, the basic properties of the soda create a chemical reaction that produces carbon dioxide, one of the same byproducts of the fermentation process when bread is made with yeast. The carbon dioxide lightens the bread, which can be baked with whole meal flour, which includes not just the starch from the wheat (such as in all-purpose flour) but also the germ and the bran. It is even hardier than whole wheat flour. The baking soda also lends a particular minerality to the bread.

According to food historians, commercial yeast wasn't readily available to the poor Irish in the mid-nineteenth century. (I can't help but wonder if wild yeasts would have helped breads rise.) Many sources say that it was Native Americans who first discovered that soda ash used in breads and cakes baked on hot stones would leaven them. However, it wasn't until the early 1800s that baking soda was introduced in Ireland.

Food traditions are often born of necessity and availability. Famine came to Ireland in the middle of the nineteenth century. One million Irish died of hunger. At least two million more left their homeland in search of food across the Atlantic, bringing with them their recipes for soda bread that had sustained them, made with humble ingredients of flour, baking soda, salt, and buttermilk, the watery byproduct of churning butter. The dense loaves were often the only thing served for dinner during lean years on both sides of the ocean.

While the Irish Soda Bread Preservation Society (try singing that to the Kinks' "Village Green Preservation Society") may claim that *true* soda bread is just buttermilk, baking soda, salt, and flour ("anything else makes it a tea cake!" they insist), designating any kind of culinary tradition "true" or "authentic" runs the risk of undermining how these food traditions are born to begin with. It also smacks of nostalgia—if not outright snobbery. As if food is not meant for all people. We simply cannot say that the evolution of a food must stop at a certain point. It took some time for even those four ingredients to be considered staples. While we can say that by the late nineteenth century the standard ingredients Irish families were using to make this staple bread were buttermilk, baking soda, salt, and flour and that to taste what they were likely tasting, you'd have to use these ingredients, soda bread continues to have a variety of forms.

THE SACRED LIFE OF BREAD

Hunger is not merely for calories. Our bodies may demand fuel, but our spirits cry out for something more. The two longings are often impossible to delineate. There's something spiritual at stake when we talk about authenticity and truth in our history. Why else would a rock 'n' roll band from the 1960s have sung "God save Tudor houses, antique tables, and billiards," a sort of prayer for a generation experiencing cultural shifts at a rate faster than ever before in human history? History is an anchor that we tether ourselves to. And knowing that anchor is firmly lodged in the sand, in the murky depths of an ocean of stories we can never truly, completely know, gives us a sense of both safety and connectedness to those stories, even if only the edges of them are whispered across generations. In a raging sea stirred by wind and tides, the crew of a ship battered by waves and pelting rain at least knows they will not be thrown off course. An anchored ship that survives a stormy night can get back to its route when the sun breaks and the sea is calm.

I have an old recipe book my aunt handed on to me. She and I have discovered that we're the throughlines of our family's food history, the ones who will obsessively pore over recipes or seek out ingredients. I waited until my forties to receive such sacred scripture. The book is stuffed with crisp sheets of yellowed paper, scrawled in elegant cursive handwriting that looks similar to but not quite the same as my grandmother's. Recipes are written in the book itself, but those sections tabbed Bread, Cakes, Candies, and Desserts, as well as Eggs, Fish, Ices, Jellies, and Oysters, a testament to the culinary expectations the mid-century culture had of housewives, are largely missing entries. It's the quickly jotted-down notes on index cards, typed onto plain paper with a handwritten "To Mary (my great-grandmother) from Helen (perhaps my great-grandfather's sister)" that fill out the collection. There is even a recipe for marble cake written onto a notepad from a casket salesman. I'm taken by how many of the recipes are for breads, cakes, and muffins—all hints that my interest in baking is not anomalous in my family.

When my aunt gave me the book, I looked for a recipe for soda bread hoping to find an alternative to the one my mother sent me written in my youthful hand. I found it in my grandmother's writing and compared it to the one my mother had been using. The two recipes are identical. The ingredients are even in the same order, which is to say, in no order at all that pertains to the directions. It also proves we've been forcing ourselves to enjoy a bread that is simply not good for a very long time.

The last time I made my family's Irish Bread, I omitted the raisins. I then slathered thick hunks of it with Kerrygold butter and layered sliced tomatoes and aged cheddar on top. But the flavor of the caraway seeds continued to dominate, and worse, the baking powder declared its all-pervasive presence in a chalky, strange aftertaste that almost burned. Not even good butter, sharp cheese, and bright tomatoes covered its offensives. The bread was dense. Not brick-like, and certainly not dry; there was enough sour cream and butter to keep the bread soft. It was just heavy in the mouth—and belly. I used freshly opened baking powder, so I knew the problem wasn't the ingredient. It was how much of it I used.

IRISH SODA BREAD

Irish Bread hints at who I am, how I am, why I am, but I knew I could make it better. The question was, could I do it while also nodding with respect to the recipe that my family has sworn by my whole life? Was it possible to make right the sins of this old family recipe? Would it lose authenticity and become a bread we call Irish but no longer deserves to be?

Ironically, it was when I finally decided to change the recipe and embrace "inauthenticity" that I discovered a much deeper connection to my grandmother and her mother, to my aunts, and to all the women whose feet touched the soil of that island across the sea. They left in search of food. This is just food. Why not make it delicious and worth making and eating year-round? When I told a friend about my desire to change a family recipe, she remarked, "To transcend our histories, we have to name the bad. And it starts with soda bread."

CRANBERRY-ORANGE IRISH BREAD

Makes 1 loaf

Soda bread by anyone else's description, this bread is my family's link to the past. In revising it, I've attempted to maintain that link. The cranberries recall driving through Cape Cod with my grandparents to see the bogs filled with the tart fruits. The caraway seeds are optional, but they are a nod to my grandmother's version, which was redolent with them, and when coupled with the orange zest, the two dance well together in an Irish jig kind of way.

2½ cups (500 g) all-purpose flour

1 teaspoon baking soda

½ teaspoon salt

¼ cup (50 g) sugar

1 teaspoon caraway seeds

zest of 2 oranges

3½ tablespoons butter, chilled and diced

½ cup dried cranberries

1 egg, lightly beaten

¾ cup buttermilk

1. Preheat the oven to 400°F. Either butter a 5-inch cast-iron skillet (a deep "fry pan" if you have one) or line a baking sheet with parchment.

2. In a large bowl, stir together flour, baking soda, salt, sugar, caraway seeds, and orange zest. Add the butter, rubbing it into the flour mixture until it resembles coarse sand. Add the dried cranberries and mix.

3. Add the egg and the buttermilk and stir to form a sticky, shaggy dough. Let it sit a minute to allow the dough to hydrate. Turn it directly into the skillet or onto the parchment and quickly shape into a ball, and flatten lightly with your hand. Transfer dough to the parchment-lined baking sheet or into the greased skillet. Using a bench cutter or knife, score into quarters pressing nearly all the way to the bottom of the loaf (do not go all the way through).

4. Bake for 30 minutes or until cooked through and golden. Cool on a wire rack for 30 minutes. Spread slices with good butter and enjoy.

ANCIENT

MY FRIEND JEFFREY SENDS ME A picture taken with his phone of his most recent loaf of sourdough. "It's 100 percent whole grain," he informs me. Even more, the flours he's used are of ancient varieties of wheat, some so old they're mentioned in the Bible: black emmer, einkorn, and spelt. He bakes a loaf about once a week, maintaining his practice in an almost monkish way—which makes sense as he spent several years living in community with Franciscan brothers.

I envy Jeffrey for his commitment to the routine exercises of tending to his starter and baking regularly, among his other spiritual-like practices of fermenting vegetables and fruits and foraging for mushrooms and various grasses and herbs that grow wild in the forest preserves around Chicago. He has to do this surreptitiously, of course, as the city does not sanction this rummaging for edible plants on municipal property. I joined him once in early spring. We didn't find any mushrooms to eat. We did clip small bunches of lemony wood sorrel, stinging nettle, and garlicky chives, as well as a large mushroom cap that I took home to my son to make mushroom art at Jeffrey's insistence. You turn a mushroom cap over onto a sheet of clean paper, he says, so that the gills are facing down and place a glass over the top. We tried it and after several hours undisturbed, the mushroom's spores settled in delicate but precise lines that revealed the exquisite patterns of the gills. I was reminded yet again of how the quiet humility of nature can conceal its extraordinary beauty.

The loaf he's just snapped is golden and lofty, carefully scored in a single cut down the center where the dough has expanded and then sprung upward and outward in a sudden rush of life in the oven. Baked to a golden brown, it is now fixed in time. A cast memory of the moment in which the yeast offered the last of their breath and the blazing heat of the oven transformed dough into bread. I am amazed. Even the spendy loaves I've purchased at a nearby bakery are smaller and denser. I've not managed to get that sort of oven spring with my own loaves baked with only half whole wheat flour, half the ever reliable, high-protein bread flour.

I begin to respond in a flurry of emojis signaling my awe but then think otherwise. Instead, I ask him to share his secrets and describe his method. Method, rather than recipe, is how most serious bread bakers I know work. They don't think so much in precise amounts of each ingredient, despite the conventional wisdom that says otherwise; they think in terms of ratios of water to flour.

He's rather nonchalant about it all. This is a practice, after all, and not some new discovery. He texts me to say how he's been baking lately, including the amount in grams of starter, water, and flours, which he describes more or less as a little of this and a little of that. We communicate in a baker's language, me jotting down notes by hand in my notebook, half delighting in our shared secret language, half wondering if this magic only works in his kitchen.

Jeffrey has a fondness for the wisdom of the past, especially wisdom that takes its cues from the natural world. He is curious about how things once were, in untold stories from yesteryear, and how, when we remember them, they might come alive again. When we first met, it was because I was offering a presentation in which I reflected on how, in the processes that create bread and wine, the elements used for a holy feast during our Sunday liturgical celebrations, offer spiritual insights that can only enrich our understanding of that holy feast. In talking afterward, we discovered that we both are delighted by how the aroma of a simple sourdough starter, an ancient formula of flour, water, and the wild yeasts that float most abundantly in the air of a kitchen where bread is baked regularly, whispers of unripe peaches, fresh cut grass, or golden straw laid out on a barnyard floor. He discovered the ancient grains from this particular loaf of bread he shared after I excitedly gushed about where he could buy them at a reasonable price. "I've switched all my flour," he told me. "This stuff just tastes so much fresher. You can taste the land." (Jeffrey doesn't gush like I tend to gush over new discoveries. His glee is more like a steady stream, the consequence of a life lived in monkish prayerful, meditative routine.)

The past bears a double-edged sword. It's not all wisdom and good sense. The past contains deep wounds, too, some of which have left scars and some of which haven't stopped bleeding. My conversation with Jeffrey lights up images in my mind of old wood-fired hearths. Peasant bread made of rye and barley, dark and dense. Round *pain au levain* scented by the smoke of the oven fire and bronzed and slightly singed on its thick crust. Round beads of sweat along the hairline of the baker as he pulls loaves from the blazing hearth with a long, wooden peel. The images are beautiful, but I bet that baker would have loved my gas-powered oven in my climate-controlled home. Unromantic, perhaps, but they are rather useful for preventing fire and heat stroke.

There is the past's wisdom, yes, but there is also modern refrigeration. And I make very good use of it for storing stone-milled flour, which keeps it fresh even in my west-facing apartment kitchen where the afternoon summer sun can jack up the heat by several degrees, despite drawn solar curtains. I keep two ten-pound bags of flour in one of the crisper drawers and several three- and five-pound bags of flour ground from various grains on the bottom shelf.

And save for a few weeks in the height of a global health pandemic, flour has always been readily available in my lifetime. I didn't even go to the grocery store to buy the flour in my fridge. I didn't trudge through mud to the town mill to retrieve it. It arrived at my front door. I just had to carry it up the stairs to my apartment, a task that, let's be honest, I relegated to my husband. (I will give up my feminist card to be spared lugging heavy loads up four flights of stairs with this weary, post-childbirth back.)

Then there is the starter, which, when I'm not baking regularly, also lives in the fridge, nestled in the back, behind plenty of milk, butter, and homemade yogurt, and a couple pieces of sockeye salmon that I'm defrosting for dinner, frozen right on the boat where the fish was caught and shipped, then mailed, again, to my door, *from Alaska*. Yes, the past has wisdom, but so does the present.

We can acknowledge the wisdom of the past, but we ought to keep a critical eye in order to prevent our reverence for what once was from becoming nostalgia, lest what once *was* outsizes what *could be*. When we become nostalgic, we risk seeing in one hue only: rose. Nostalgia, at best, eliminates all other colors. At worst, it sees and ignores anyway. It interprets the present only in comparison to the past—a past that never was as we see it now. It lacks imagination and does not allow for optimistic pondering of what might be: an abundance of all things good and wonderful for all people. A world where there is not just enough but a bounty of equity, peace, love, joy—and bread.

Nostalgia for the past looms large in the spiritual lives of not just Christians but many practitioners of religion, thanks to the fact that most of the world's religions have ancient roots. There is both benefit and risk to tug backward. Ancient wisdom can be a candle that illuminates the present. On the other hand, if we're not careful, we can wander into the territory of nostalgia, which doesn't so much offer light as it snuffs out the glow of the present. Oddly, Christians don't tend to get nostalgic for the time of Jesus—rather, we do tend to romanticize eras when the church dominated all of life, when there was no division between secular and sacred, such as the Middle Ages. It is, I suspect, the cultural dominance of the past that Christians of today long for.

Churchgoers young and old where I serve confide in me that our weekly celebration, with its deliberately slow choreography, yesteryear's music, and vestments that harken back to medieval royalty, is a relief from the quickness with which the world seems to want to move on from religion. Out there, "they" ignore the past that we know to be important. Outside of our sanctuary with its stained glass and candles, no one seems to take seriously the wisdom of what is old and ancient. Out there, we're laughed at for wanting to kneel in humility in front of a piece of bread.

I am sympathetic but cautious. The past is often considered the home of silly superstitions, laughably wrong science, sexism, and, of course, ridiculous religion. And many Christians can't seem to help themselves in perpetuating the myth that faith amounts to checking your brain at the church's door rather than drawing on an ancient people's wisdom for how to live in the present with an eye to a glorious future for the generations to come. But the past is not a refuge from the present, no matter how often we nod to it in our most sacred spaces.

Religion is not the only one of life's arenas where nostalgia chokes the present of meaning and the future of progress. A recent former US president continues to boldly proclaim how he and his political regime would usher in what was once great about America. As if things have gone off the rails for our country and what it needs is a return to the things of the past, when everything was just as it should be. Just four words, a campaign slogan that has since infiltrated hearts and minds, betray a blindness. Those words envision a painting in one color only. Whether intentional or woefully myopic, they block out resplendent color, light, and shadow. They see not a complex portrait of a multitude of brushstrokes that convey pain, suffering, loss, injustice, triumph, justice, and joy but a whitewashed canvas.

There is wisdom to be gleaned from the past, but we'll never see its light if we look only at earlier eras under the floodlights of the present. When I celebrate the Eucharist, an ancient rite where a meal of bread and wine are blessed, I tell an old story and twice recall the words of a Palestinian Jew who said some two thousand years ago: "Do this in memory of me." I then elevate a piece of bread for the community gathered to ponder that ancient meal and its significance for us today. The power of the past in that moment is not in how closely we can reenact it but in how recalling it we draw closer to God right here, right now. We become more who we are in the present and are reminded of what we can be as we go forward into the future.

I love to bake with ancient grains. Like Jeffrey, I find that it makes my breads taste fresh and interesting. I even tip one of my favorites, black emmer, milled from grains of farro that supposedly have genetic ancestry to the grains grown in ancient Egypt (*farro* comes from *Pharoah*), into pancake batter on a Saturday morning.

The swell of interest in "wellness" has led to more popularity of such grains as well as the predictable "well, actually," from critics who claim that the moniker of "ancient" is marketing only and not rooted in fact. So-called ancient grains, they say, are no substitute for the hardy, high-yielding wheat strains used for most flour found on grocery store shelves. I'm not an expert in nutrition or even the history of food, but I do think there's something real at stake for farmers, bakers, or bread lovers who long for a way to connect with the farms, kitchens, and breads of the past and to allow the wisdom of the past to have a bearing on our collective future.

The tension between sensibilities old and new is palpable in our approach to politics, the arts and sciences, and our education systems. Things change, whether or not we want them to. Nothing stays the same in this dynamic and living world we inhabit. It is as terribly frustrating as it is incredibly exciting. But we also cannot throw out the past simply because it is old. One of the great things about ancient grains is that they offer variety, which means different kinds of flavor and textures when baking with them.

Because we are a people firmly situated in time, we are always negotiating our past with our future. We once were there. Now we are here. Where will we be next? I don't think we can only respond reactively, defending why we cannot change certain things, when faced with the future, which, as people of the present, is always. We cannot be unmovable stones, for even the stones are worn away, eroded in the passage of time. We also cannot forget our history and who we were and how we got to this point. History matters. It is a lens through which to understand who we are, as people now.

One of the things I love about baking is how thoroughly impractical it is. If you add up the amount of time spent planning, gathering ingredients—and, in the case of special-ordered ancient grains, waiting for them to arrive— baking, and cooling, you're better off purchasing an artisan loaf at a nearby bakery. The cost of ingredients and time spent baking at home simply outweigh the value of the finished product, no matter how delicious. I once read an essay by a former professional baker who is now the test kitchen manager for *Saveur* magazine: "Truth- fully, it is not practical to make most types of bread at home," she wrote. "Crusty rustic loaves can take days to create, and unless scheduled into a professional bakery's daily rhythm, the time and effort involved in making a loaf or two just doesn't make sense—particularly for the average busy family with a decent neighborhood bakery nearby."

I'm not convinced that the average busy family outside of a metropolis has a decent neighborhood bakery nearby (the *Saveur* author lived in New York City), nor am I convinced by what "makes sense." It depends on what you're after. Our modern sensibilities certainly value efficiency of time spent. We measure success in terms of big outcomes achieved in as little time as possible. No wonder religion is in decline.

Baking bread at home may not be your calling if you are busy and want to stay that way. Spending hours carefully measuring out ingredients and puttering around the house while waiting for your dough to rise or finish baking is impractical if you are busy and wish to stay that way. If bread is simply food and food is simply physical nourishment meant to power your time-efficient days, then, yes, it will always make more sense to purchase your bread from a grocery store or neighborhood bakery, even if the bread costs eight dollars a loaf (less than an hour at minimum wage and pretty good if that loaf of bread is used for toast, sandwiches, and dunking in soup for a family of four).

But if you seek something more than high yields for your time, bake bread at home in an act of defiance. Gather the ancient grains that required more work to grow and knead the dough by hand if you're able and want to discover the truths of what bakers before you learned. Immerse yourself in the deep and ancient patterns of a practice that yields more than a simple loaf of bread.

PIZZA DOUGH WITH BLACK EMMER

Adapted from Smitten Kitchen

Yields 2 12-inch round pizzas

*That we can bake out of joy and not only
necessity is quite a modern phenomenon.
Baking with ancient grains (or, at least, grains
with DNA dating back to ancient times) in a
kitchen with modern amenities is pure delight
and thanks to past generations who allowed
their imaginations of the future to run wild.*

*This is an all-day recipe. Mix the dough in
the morning before starting your day. Black
emmer can be ordered online from places such
as Janie's Mill. If you can't get your hands on*

it, whole wheat works just fine, but it's worth seeking out the grain of ancient Egypt.

---

2 cups (250 g) all-purpose flour

1 cup (130 g) black emmer flour (can substitute with whole wheat)

¼ teaspoon rounded, active dry yeast (1.42 g if your scale will measure that precisely)

1½ teaspoons sea salt

1¼ cups (270 g) water, plus 2 tablespoons as needed

---

1. Combine all the ingredients in a large bowl using a spoon or, even better, a Danish dough hook. It will be a rough mixture, but if it looks too dry, add a tablespoon or two of water. Keep in mind that as it sits, the dough will hydrate, so be careful not to add too much more water.

2. Cover and leave it to rise all day until more than doubled, approximately 12 hours.

3. Arrange a rack in the bottom third of the oven. At least 30 minutes before baking, preheat your oven to its highest setting, around 500°F or 550°F and place a pizza stone, if using, on the bottom rack.

4. Generously flour a work surface and tip the dough out. It will be very soft, sticky and stretchy. Sprinkle a little flour over the top and divide in half using a bench scraper or knife. With floured hands, shape each piece into something that resembles a ball. The dough will be pretty slack, and so will not get perfectly round.

5. Lay out a sheet of parchment on a baking sheet or pizza peel and spray lightly with oil. One piece at a time, transfer the dough to the peel or sheet and work into a round or rectangular shape by nudging, pulling, and draping the dough.

6. Prepare with toppings as desired (a quick recipe for pizza sauce follows) and bake for 10 to 15 minutes. Repeat with the second piece.

LAST-MINUTE PIZZA SAUCE

1. Whisk together a 5-ounce can tomato paste with 1 cup water, 1 tablespoon olive oil, and 1 teaspoon each kosher salt, dried oregano, and dried basil. Refrigerate for 1 week or freeze leftovers.

A COMMON LOAF

SHORTLY AFTER MY HUSBAND AND I returned to church after three years away, we decided to baptize our kid. We met with one of the priests, a friend of mine, about holding this celebration on Albie's first birthday, because that's when some family would be in town anyway. My priest friend asked me if I'd be willing to bake communion bread for the celebration. He knew I was a decent baker and sensed that it would be a meaningful opportunity for me. I agreed. This, I could do. This would take very little of my energy and would indeed feel very meaningful to bake the bread we'd share with this new community.

"It has to be gluten-free," my friend added. The other priest who would be presiding had celiac disease and couldn't even touch bread made with wheat. My own husband was in a trial period of abstaining from wheat after some persistent health issues led him to wonder if he was having a reaction to the wheat in his diet. But I'd not yet ventured into gluten-free baking. We just ate food that was naturally gluten-free: tacos instead of sandwiches, rice instead of pasta.

Communion bread needs to be tearable for sharing small pieces without creating a big mess and dunking into wine without deteriorating into soggy crumbs. Gluten-free bread is especially prone to both of those things. Still, I was up for the challenge. I'd eaten freshly baked communion bread before and knew how spectacular it could be. I had a flavor in mind inspired from a particularly delicious portion of communion bread that I still cannot get off my mind. It was sweet and slightly nutty, really enjoyable, the way bread should always be.

Another friend pointed me toward a recipe they'd once read about in the *Christian Century*. There, the writers shared their desire for a gluten-free bread that would accommodate those allergic to nightshades (potato flour was out) and vegans (no eggs, no milk, no honey). After a few test bakes, I turned out several pretty delicious loaves of bread. I still could not achieve that pronounced flavor of honey I'd sought, but with the interesting blend of flours—a fava/chickpea blend, teff, brown rice, sweet rice, and tapioca—I'd managed to get real flavor, not the wet sponge texture and taste of so much gluten-free bread. It had rise and texture and chew and even a crisp crust. It tasted nourishing and paired well with fortified communion wine. The recipe was a winner.

Well, sort of. Immediately after my son's baptism, the questions started rolling in. What was in the bread? (A mix of gluten-free flours.) Why didn't you use eggs like most gluten-free breads? (I wanted to make it vegan.) What was that crunchy stuff on the bottom? (Cornmeal to prevent it from sticking to the baking stone in the oven.) And so on.

My friend had thought that by introducing a freshly baked loaf of bread to the parish at a baptism, something special and out of the ordinary, that the congregation would take to it like bees to honey and want it every week. But it turned out the rector also didn't do well digesting beans, and this bread had a fair amount of fava and chickpea flours. Many parishioners were confused when offered a torn piece of brown bread instead of a pale communion wafer and didn't know what to do about dunking it in the wine (which is honestly one of the most unsanitary practices—it's not just bread, but fingers, that take a dip—and it should be avoided). The committee that set up the altar for church every week was likewise thrown off because they didn't know what to do about counting wafers for communion the following Sunday.

Here I had achieved the unachievable, a common loaf of bread to be broken and shared

by a community that accommodated a wide
range of dietary restrictions: gluten, dairy, egg,
and nightshades. In a single loaf of bread was a
potent symbol of unity, far more powerful than
a container of papery wafers and a second small
packet of rice crackers from Trader Joe's for the
gluten-free folks. We could all share this bread
together despite our various needs. I had sought
a common loaf of communion bread that accommodated the needs of an entire parish. And yet,
the bread turned out to be disruptive.

It was also disruptive to my wallet, which
was always in the process of being emptied by
the cost of childcare. Specialty flours are expensive. Later, after a few more months had elapsed
and people had gradually warmed to the idea of
baking gluten-free vegan communion bread, I
was encouraged to start a bread guild. But the
parish didn't have a budget for the expensive
ingredients. I didn't want to admit that I couldn't
afford to keep making this bread. Plus, the recipe
was too fussy. It needed the hand of someone
who really knew bread and then was willing to

ignore some of those instincts, not a group of volunteers willing to follow a recipe. The bread, even for me, didn't always come out right. Then there was the issue of whether or not we could actually call it gluten-free when it was made in a kitchen where wheat flour was also used.

It didn't take me long to finally understand the appeal of communion wafers.

After making bread two or three more times for my church, I started to wonder if the words *community* and *accommodate* had the same root. I looked them up in an extra-large dictionary. I had hoped that the root of the latter would be "common," as in to make accessible, more common, to be shared among more people.

I was wrong. The root of *accommodate* is *commod*, which means to make fit or suiting. My inner ten-year-old giggled. I knew down to my soul that this made good sense because so often the hard work of accommodating others really can feel like throwing all good intentions into the toilet. Have a great idea, then try to fit it to others' expectations, wants, and needs, and where did that idea even go? The toilet. Even when starting with the idea of accommodating, as I did with the allergy- and dietary-preferences-aware common loaf of communion bread, had I managed to accommodate absolutely everyone's dietary burdens? Unlikely. And even on that rare occasion when everyone's *needs* have been accommodated, the wants will not be. If only we were all the same and easy to please. If only "if only's" were worth anything at all.

Still, I do believe with my heart and soul that it is always worth the bother of trying anyway. Because the attempts at accommodating others' diversity of needs, and even some wants, can be transformative, life changing.

Some years ago, I began a friendship with Kelly, whom I now consider one of my dearest friends. We had been brought together by mutual acquaintances: other mothers who shared a similar approach to being mothers in that we were uninterested in parenting styles at all. We didn't consider the fact that we have children to be what defines us. It's not easy to find other mothers whose company you need because of the distinct shared experience of caring for children who also don't lead with "I'm Johnny's mom," when introducing themselves. And so, we shared a common experience that was not so common that it set the boundaries of our friendship—to the contrary, it gave us the common ground that allowed for us to talk about things unrelated to our progeny.

I knew from the occasional quips and comments about Christians, that I was probably the only one of us who still found value in institutional religion. So it was with vulnerability that I eventually shared with my "mom friends" that I was wondering about becoming an Episcopal priest. Kelly told me that she was an Episcopalian, too. She'd been raised an atheist, was (and still is) married to a brilliant physicist, and still wasn't so sure about how she felt about God. But she wandered into a church during a period of deep pain and sadness in her life, longing not for explanations or even solace. It was a place to not have answers but to be with others—in all their murkiness and differences. It was and continues to be a place to share in the common experiences of pain and joy, sadness and celebration. "The Eucharist is it for me," Kelly confided one day. "Me, too," I responded. We then went on and on to each other about how special this meal was. In all our variety, here was a sign of unity, a way for us to come together and belong to one another.

Intellectually, she and I and so many others I know wrestle with what it means that we count ourselves among the faithful, Christians who, in the name of Jesus, ostracize and marginalize anyone who challenges their power. How can we call ourselves followers of the same religion as those churchgoers who so repulse us (and whom we also certainly repulse)? I'm not sure that we do. But our claim to what we call Christian is apparent in the celebration of the Eucharist: simple bread and wine around a table.

Not long after this conversation, Kelly was tested for celiac disease and learned that for the sake of her health, she had to give up bread made with wheat. She was devastated. I mourned for her, having witnessed and gone through a similar break-up with wheat when a few years prior my husband learned that his body, too, was rejecting the bread I'd been baking. Now they're both relegated to rice crackers for communion, which are better for them but are a pale substitute for a piece of freshly baked bread.

The stakes of the form that communion bread takes seem low, but I'm not sure they are. I think we who practice this ritual can do better to accommodate others, and not just to bend to dietary fashions, as they're seen by naysayers who get exasperated when asked if there's a gluten-free option. The symbol or sign of bread broken and shared conceals the very unity it's meant to convey.

An elderly man from my church, whom I'll call Clifford, lives alone even though he is in his mid-nineties and probably would do much better in an assisted living facility. But he is (mostly) capable of managing the demands of daily life and too poor to afford such accommodations. He takes the bus to church every week, showing up so, well, religiously, that when I didn't see him in the front pew one Sunday, I got nervous. After too-many-to-count fruitless attempts to contact him by phone, I showed up to his apartment building, only to discover that the building's intercom system connects to his home phone number, which, every time I rang it, bleakly told me that the number was not available and I should call back later. Then came a well-being check, accompanied by police officers, and after knocking on his door repeatedly, Clifford, who is mostly deaf, finally appeared.

His phone had been shut off when he came up short of the additional thirty dollars the phone company started charging him to accommodate their new and "improved" service updates. Easy enough, I thought. I have a small discretionary fund I can dip into to meet just such needs as this. Only Clifford no longer had a copy of the bill. I went to the phone company's website and discovered I could pay the bill without a bill. I just needed the phone number. I applied a generous amount to his account to pay for several months of phone service.

What ensued, when his phone still would not come back on, was a seemingly endless loop of customer service agents who could not get past the question, "What is the passcode?" Clifford had no recollection of ever creating a passcode, not because of his failing memory (which was actually quite sharp) but because he'd never created one. "OK, I understand," the third, fourth, fifth woman in a call center across the globe told me as I explained *yet again* that there was no passcode. "My manager Mark will be able to help you." The first thing Mark asked me? "What is the account's four-digit passcode?" The details of this unfolding drama are the stuff of a modern retelling of Dante's *Inferno*, the section on the seventh circle of hell.

Reader, this is not a story about how I, a scrappy, can-do priest, relentless in my quest for justice and compassion for the most marginalized members of society, got Clifford's phone service reinstated. I wish it were. I suffer from insomnia, and when his social worker texted me late on a Friday night, just as I had finally fallen asleep (and forgotten to set my phone to Do Not

A COMMON LOAF

Disturb), to tell me that she was unable to get his phone working, I confess to a brief moment in which I wished the Lord would take him—not to relieve Clifford of this cruel world that no longer had room for him, but to relieve me.

This is why I go to a table week after week to celebrate the Eucharist. This is why the Eucharist is *it* for me. Without it, I might start to think that it would be OK to be relieved of the burden of having to accommodate others in their time of deepest need. Breaking bread around a table, in the name and in communion with God and others, means Clifford always has a seat. This table will always make room for him, even if the rest of the world no longer wants to accommodate him because he is too cumbersome. He is too old, too deaf, too poor, and we don't have room for that kind of need is the sentiment I kept encountering in those phone calls with customer service. They simply didn't have a script for how to help, even if they wanted to.

The prayers I offer when I preside at a Eucharist are that script. Around this table, everyone fits, even if we're not always (or ever) great at accommodating all the needs that come to it. This script, as imperfect as it is, in our words and our voices, tells us how to pull up more chairs and make the table even bigger.

If we allow the boundaries of our own needs and wants as they are right now to confine us, what will happen when we find ourselves outside those lines and on the margins? And so, I press on with the untidy task of trying to make sure there's bread for everyone. I am not usually successful, but I hope the trying is what counts and what points the way.

GLUTEN-FREE, VEGAN COMMUNION BREAD

The flours in this bread are admittedly not your average gluten-free flour blends. They can be purchased online and often found in health stores. The same goes for the psyllium husks, which when combined with the chia seeds give this bread the necessary sturdiness for tearing and dipping in communion wine.

If not baking communion bread, bake a single loaf for 40 minutes and share as you would a basket of bread made with wheat. It is especially good slathered with butter or used to mop up the bottom of a bowl of soup.

2½ cups warm water

2¼ teaspoons active dry yeast (1 package)

1 teaspoon sugar

1 cup gluten-free oat flour

1 cup tapioca flour

½ cup sweet rice flour

½ cup teff flour

1½ teaspoons salt

2 tablespoons maple syrup

2 tablespoons olive oil

⅓ cup ground chia seeds (can also use ⅓ cup ground poppy or sesame seeds)

⅓ cup whole psyllium husks

1. Whisk together the warm water and yeast. Let it rest for 5 to 10 minutes to activate the yeast. (It should look foamy on the surface of the water. If not, try again with another packet of yeast.) While yeast is activating,

whisk together in a large bowl oat, tapioca, sweet rice, and teff flours. Add the salt.

2. When the yeast is ready, whisk in the maple syrup, olive oil, chia seeds, and whole psyllium husks. Let the mixture stand for 2 to 3 minutes. Then whisk again. It will be rather thick.

3. Pour the wet ingredients into the dry ingredients and mix with a wooden spoon until it all comes together. Knead, adding oat or teff flour, a little at a time, until the dough stays together and is just slightly sticky.

4. Form the dough into a ball, place in a large oiled bowl, and cover with a damp towel or plastic wrap. Let it rise in a warm place for 1 to 2 hours, or until doubled in size. When the dough is risen, place a pizza stone in the center of the oven and preheat to 400°F. Place a pan of water in the bottom of the oven.

5. Punch the dough down and knead for 1 minute. Then form into 2 to 4 small loaves

and place on lightly oiled parchment. Use a sharp knife to cut a cross into each loaf, then brush with olive oil. Cover loosely with plastic wrap and allow to proof until puffy for 30 minutes.

6. Using the parchment, slide the loaves directly onto the pizza stone. Bake for 35 minutes. Remove from the oven and cool completely.

7. To store communion bread, you can wrap each loaf in plastic wrap and place it in a freezer bag. Store in the refrigerator if you plan to use it within 2 days, otherwise freeze it and then defrost a day before it is needed.

SANDWICHES

MY DEVOTION TO LAYERING ANY-
thing and everything between two slices of bread
became a sort of badge of honor when I was a
child. From it came one of my earliest experiences of identity. "You are definitely a Meehan,"
my grandfather would remark while watching
me mound spaghetti Bolognese on a buttered
slice of soft white bread to roll over. "Meehans
can turn anything into a sandwich." We were
seated at the Formica table in my grandparents'
kitchen. My memories of this time in my life are
hued in the earth tones of the early 1980s. In my
recollection, the tabletop was rusty orange, and
the kitchen cabinets were dark brown; the lino-
leum tiles were all yellow-ochre, unlike in today's

kitchens where bright white and stainless steel dominates.

With this sense of identity girding me like armor against all raised eyebrows and sharp gasps, I felt completely free to experiment. Scrambled eggs most certainly had to be eaten with grape jelly smooshed between two triangles of buttered toast. This was especially important if the eggs were overcooked and/or under seasoned. Salad sandwiches made salads, well, more like sandwiches and therefore more enjoyable to eat. The same went for meatloaf, the flavor of which I had to disguise by covering it in mashed potatoes and rolling it all in a soft slice of bread.

During the summers when I visited my dad, I'd rifle through cabinets in search of a tasty and satisfying snack to dissolve my boredom for at least fifteen minutes. I settled on bacon bits and crunchy peanut butter—a lazy and less sweet take on a combination made famous by Elvis Presley, who reportedly added banana slices, though at the time and for decades I thought I was the only one in the world who knew the virtues of combining peanut butter with salty bacon (or bacon-flavored pieces of whatever bacon bits are made of).

I also love the classics, the beloved combinations found in nearly every spot that calls itself a sandwich shop. Turkey club. BLT. Ham and Swiss. Peanut butter and jelly (so long as the potato chips lie inside, not alongside, the sandwich).

These days, I grow tomatoes in the summer on my back porch. West facing, the back of my apartment gets a direct hit from the afternoon, late-afternoon, and evening sun, until that glowing orb finally and blessedly dips behind a neighbor's tree. The sun is so intense in the summer that we had to install special solar shades for our windows. Without them, the heat was overwhelming our air conditioner. Even without the heat, the sun reflects off the smooth, hardwood floors, blinding anyone who accidentally glances in the direction of its rays. It is the perfect location for growing tomatoes.

That is, when they have enough water. During the first summer of the pandemic, Andrew converted two thirty-something-gallon bins into self-irrigating planters for my tomatoes. To fill the bins, however, we had to make multiple trips back and forth from the kitchen sink, lugging two three-gallon watering cans. Four stories up, the kitchen sink is our only water supply. And those tomatoes can drink some serious water. Two afternoons in the blazing August sun, and the plants can look to be on the verge of death by wilting. That first summer, all the schlepping proved worthwhile. My tomatoes, always the smaller cherry- and grape-sized varieties, were tastier and more abundant than they'd ever been before.

The second summer of the pandemic, I planted Brandywine tomatoes for the first time. For years, I'd stuck to cherry tomatoes, happy to harvest bowls of ten to thirty tomatoes at a time all summer long. For at least four weeks anyway—about how long it takes me to fatigue of tomatoes in and on and next to breakfast, lunch, and dinner. The copy on the back of the seed packet promised large, juicy tomatoes perfect for slicing for sandwiches. I was sold.

I nurtured tiny tomato sprouts into seedlings, playing the cruel role of Mother Nature as I thinned back the sprouts and seedlings that looked less likely to produce healthy, strong plants. In the end, from about thirty plants, only five were left. About twenty-five died in the early spring sun when I'd left them out back for too long while hardening them off. I kept one and placed the other four in a cardboard box next to a little library on our corner. My son drew a sign: Free tomato plants!

By the time late August rolled around, the one plant had produced seven fist-sized green tomatoes that blushed into, appropriately, tomato red, first one by one and then suddenly all at once. I'd walked outside one morning to check on the plants to discover that first perfectly ripe tomato and knew what I had to do. With no time to bake a fresh loaf of bread, I sent my husband out for store-bought brioche. If we were to enjoy that tomato perfect for slicing for sandwiches at its absolute peak and not on its decline into something more appropriate for sauce or soup, we needed a loaf of bread now.

At our nearest grocery store, he found a European-style brioche so rich it threatened to collapse into a stick of butter if not handled delicately. I sawed through it gently and laid the slices into a dry cast-iron skillet, where they toasted. While I waited, flipping them once freckled golden brown on the side, I unscrewed a jar of mayonnaise and cut the tomato into quarter-inch-thick medallions.

Some find the flavor of summer captured in a caprese salad—the sweet herbal basil and mild creamy mozzarella balancing bright, acidic height-of-summer tomatoes. And others claim it's in a cold glass of rosé sipped on a porch or sidewalk café in fading daylight. Salty hot dogs charred on the grill and tucked into a pillowy soft roll and washed down with an icy lager. Popsicles that drip down your chin in any flavor as long as it's sweet.

SANDWICHES

For me, it's the tomato sandwich. So simple, it's practically pedestrian. To bite into sliced tomatoes seasoned with salt and pepper between two slices of toasted bread slathered with mayonnaise is to taste the divine power of creation. Of bounty. Of long days. Of light and heat.

The humble tomato sandwich is unadorned and accessible. I love it on toasted brioche, but even the most inexpensive white sandwich bread from the grocery store will do. It needs nothing more. No bacon or lettuce. Avocados are delicious, yes, but unnecessary.

I once attended a talk given by one of my favorite theologians in which she described Christ as the first tomato of summer, a reference to Paul's letter to the Corinthians in which he describes Christ as the first fruits of those who have fallen asleep. The first tomato of summer always tastes best, doesn't it? It is the fruit of all our seasonal anticipation. I, personally, long for that first tomato before I have even planted the seedlings in the soil. Christ, this metaphor suggests, can be held by our own hands. Divine incarnate can be tasted by our own tongues.

In a good sandwich, the bread isn't an afterthought but essential to the meal. I think this is why any time in my life I've been served a roll or piece of bread "on the side" of my meal, I can't help but scoop, with gusto, the meal onto the bread. Even when I eat soup, I'm not satisfied to just dip the bread. I make a soup sandwich. Of course, my success depends on the type of soup. I'm practiced, however, having turned even canned vegetable soup into sandwiches as a child: Butter your bread generously, then delicately spoon the more toothsome bits onto the bread, being careful not to soak it through. Roll the bread over and enjoy, dipping into the soup as necessary.

And then there are next-day sandwiches. Sandwiches made with leftovers taste more spectacular than the original meal. My aunt told me once that her favorite sandwich of all time was made with all of the leftover bits of a meal that my grandfather would make for the family when she was a kid: brown-and-serve sausages, cream corn (from a can), mashed potatoes, and applesauce. She'd pile it all onto soft white bread swiped with butter or margarine. "My God it was better than the meal," she whispered as if speaking of something holy. Indeed, she was.

Hearing her talk about that sandwich, I can just see my grandfather at the stove in that same earth tone–hued kitchen, thirty years at least before I ever sat at that table. My grandmother was a nurse and worked late. My grandfather had fought in World War II and delivered the mail early in the morning. (According to my family, we have my grandfather's retirement to blame for the decline of the US Postal Service.) There were five children. Bread stretched meals. Toast with breakfast means fewer eggs to scramble. Rolls with dinner means less meat to buy—and lunch the next day.

Bread turns a mishmash of odds and ends into a meal. It's like Eucharist in this way: a ragtag assortment of odd ducks and wit's-ends in need of each other, brought together by bread and mysteriously made whole. The bread is not filler, a way to stretch a meal, but essential to making the meal itself.

I'll be honest—because I'm a woman of a certain age and therefore a certain metabolism, I have attempted to live without bread. In the interest of avoiding high blood sugar that I likewise inherited from the Meehan side of my family, I have skipped rolls offered with dinner and wrapped up deli, turkey, bacon, and tomato in iceberg lettuce instead of bread. I mean no offense to the die-hard followers of keto/paleo/low-carb lifestyle, but my "lifestyle" cannot abide sandwiches without bread, because without bread we are without life. And there is no "lifestyle" without life, just another sad diet.

Sandwiches came to play another important role in my understanding of who I am in this world. The same year I turned thirty, I hosted Thanksgiving for the first time. I'd lived in Chicago for eight years and had been married for almost five. Finally, some family had decided that I was worthy of hosting for a holiday. My dad and stepmom and a cousin who'd decided to stay at school in South Bend that year for Thanksgiving descended on the two-bedroom apartment my husband and I had just moved into. I invited a handful of friends who'd also decided to stay in town.

I could tell you about the menu I spent weeks organizing, the store-specific grocery lists I'd written, the cooking schedule beginning on the weekend prior to the holiday I'd planned. In truth, it is one of my favorite memories of Thanksgiving, eclipsed only by the general recollection of Thanksgivings celebrated with the Meehans as a child and the last Thanksgiving I shared with friends just before COVID-19 pandemic. I'd beer-brined an organic, fresh turkey bought from a farm just outside of Chicago and glazed it with barley malt. The pumpkin pie featured a candied sweet-salty pepita brittle. I'd made the nutmeg-scented béchamel for the green bean casserole from scratch and crisp-fried the onions for topping. I was (and still am, actually) quite pleased with myself.

THE SACRED LIFE OF BREAD

The memory of this meal that I most cling to, however, is not of the homemade Parker house rolls or herbed compound butter, or of the simple apple tart where I'd fanned thin slices of apples into flowers. It is, instead, of how we ate leftovers the next day, standing around my kitchen island.

The apartment was chilly. We learned that weekend that it had practically no insulation—a problem in any Chicago winter and especially when temps were in the low twenties by November. And so we stood in thick socks to protect our feet from the icy kitchen tile.

The kitchen was spacious but needed more counter space. My husband had found an IKEA-made kitchen island on Craigslist just before the holiday. We stood around it: me, my husband, my dad and stepmom, and my cousin. It was an unlikely grouping. I hadn't seen my younger cousin in ten or fifteen years. I have never been particularly close to any of my thirty-some cousins on my dad's side, least of all the one who was visiting. He was in the third wave of cousins to populate that side of the family tree. I'd been in the second. Still, this grouping felt whole. It was family, if not a complete one.

The sounds of the microwave oven door opening and closing. The high-pitched beeps of numbers being punched. The dull thud of food being set out on the island. All dinner bells, signaling that precious, beloved moment: time to eat.

My husband, parents, and cousin all gathered around the island as I set the table: A roll of paper towels and just washed salad plates, big enough for sandwiches. On a cutting board, I assembled the meal. I hadn't baked bread but had purchased a loaf of sandwich bread just for this occasion. Out of the leftovers, I assembled sandwiches for this potpourri of people: a swipe of buttermilk mashed potatoes flecked with bright green chives, a layer of cornbread and cranberry stuffing followed by thin slices of the stout-brined turkey. Then a spoonful or two of mushroom-tarragon gravy, tangy thanks to the creme fraiche and spiced cranberry-orange chutney.

We didn't even say a blessing. Grace was the sounds of satisfaction as we bit into and chewed our sandwiches.

It took me years to connect the importance of that singular memory to the meaning that I was preparing a meal around a table not unlike a priest preparing a eucharistic meal at an altar. Hosting dinner has always been meaningful to me, from selecting recipes to folding napkins, cooking the meal to sitting down to it with friends and family. But when I ended up leaving my steady job as an editor to pursue freelance writing about food full time, I did it with this specific memory of serving turkey sandwiches as my lodestar: this was the representative moment of when I felt true, unmitigated joy. If I wanted to be joyful every day, I needed this memory to be my guide.

What I was experiencing in the distribution and eating of those sandwiches, I think, was true communion, holy and unexpected. A meal of thanksgiving that extended beyond a single celebration of it. We had communed only the day before, elbows bumping as we passed heaping dishes of delicious food to one another. We poured wine and then poured more wine for each other. We shared stories and we laughed, this unlikely group of friends and family who through some happy accident or miracle—one never can tell the difference—sat at a table together and ate and were filled with all that we needed: food, drink, stories, community.

And here we were in my kitchen, doing it again, not reenacting the previous day's meal, but making it new. Extending the table into a new day. We were three fewer guests but no less complete. The candles had been extinguished, and we ate by cheap fluorescent kitchen light. No tablecloth had been ironed and smoothed out, and I am certain I pulled down a roll of paper towels for napkins. And yet, this meal, not the ostensible Thanksgiving feast, that is the memory I hold most dear.

Some years later, I recounted this memory to my therapist. I'd been stuck. Unable to earn enough money food writing alone, I'd returned to that old editor job to supplement the income. Only now I had more responsibility, at work because I was in a management role and at home because I'd had a baby. And so what was meant to supplement what I really longed to do had taken over. I had less time for food—for writing about it, making it, and reading about it. Plus, something else had come up. For months, a nagging voice had situated herself in the back pew of my mind and started saying out loud what she'd been thinking for decades: "Maybe you should be a priest."

"Why are you crying?" my therapist asked as I told her in tears about the sandwiches and the paper towels and the heat I could feel in my chest when I remembered my cousin's smile. I could barely get the words out between sobs. "Are you sad?"

"No," I said, annoyed that she'd either interpreted them as such or gave me such a silly invitation to explore their true meaning, which only became apparent to me as I said the words out loud: "These aren't tears of sadness. They're tears of longing."

SANDWICHES

I'd longed to be a priest, yes, but I also longed, and still do, for that transcendent experience of community. For that quiet communion when everyone's mouth is full of delicious food and the important thing is not that we've used the fine silver or perfectly timed the arrival of the main course and the sides at the dinner table. For that sense of connectedness that runs so deep it cannot be spoken out loud.

In his "definition" of the Lord's Supper, the late Frederick Buechner writes, "To eat any meal together is to meet at the level of our most basic need. It is hard to preserve your dignity with butter on your chin or to keep your distance when asking for the tomato ketchup."

Perhaps the same is true when slapping leftovers between bread. Or when spreading mashed potatoes or peanut butter or mayonnaise across a slab of whole wheat. When layering slices of turkey, banana, or tomato and pressing them between bread and calling it a new meal. Gravy is much more likely to drip down your chin when it's been ladled over turkey on a sandwich than over turkey to be eaten with a knife and fork.

"It's also called Holy Communion," Buechner writes, "because when feeding at this implausible table, Christians believe they are communing with the Holy One himself."

I think that making and eating those sandwiches around the kitchen island was—and is—a connection to my humble heritage of poor Irish immigrants and their descendants who worked less hard to make ends meet and to feed a large family, but still hard, nonetheless. Sandwiches speak of stewardship, of making precious resources go a little further. Sandwiches, to me, are more than a thrifty way to eat dinner, but a sort of communion with my family near and far. Between bread, glorious bread, whether tomatoes or turkey, food becomes more than what it already is. It becomes a holy meal.

THE SANDWICH

Makes 1 sandwich

*After a twelve-hour drive from Chicago to my
mother's house, we arrived feeling famished.
My mother, who lives alone, never has as
much in her fridge as my family of three, but
she does keep salami, provolone, and a jar
of roasted red peppers on hand at all times.
She compiled sandwiches for us with these
ingredients on English muffins, as she had
no other bread. They were somehow more
delicious than I could have anticipated. I
started making a version on whole grain bread
to take to work, and a coworker caught on.
Soon, we started asking each other if we had*

brought The Sandwich for lunch. The nickname has stuck ever since.

---

two slices quality whole grain bread

mayonnaise

1 marinated and roasted red pepper

1 leaf romaine lettuce

provolone cheese

2 to 3 thin slices salami

garlic powder

salt and pepper

---

1. Toast the bread and generously spread with mayonnaise. On one slice of bread, layer the lettuce, followed by the roasted pepper. Sprinkle salt, pepper, and just a touch of garlic powder. Then add the cheese and salami. Top with the other slice. Cut into two triangles (rectangles are OK, if you must) and enjoy.

PRACTICE

WHEN I BAKE BREAD, IT COMPLETELY takes over. First there is the mess of the kitchen, which even the tidiest of bakers are at pains to maintain. Some of my favorite bakers suggest a mise en place before starting bread, in which every ingredient has been measured, preferably by weight down to the gram, and set out in its own individual bowl, ready to be tipped into the larger bowl when ready. Bakers who use this method insist that this is the only means to successful loaves. I don't doubt that it's the means to consistent results, but I have absolutely zero faith that I'll want to keep baking if my first step is to dirty every bowl I have in my kitchen. This is a method for a professional kitchen, in my opinion,

205

one with a good dishwasher—both a machine and a human on the payroll.

Admittedly, I take my chances with each loaf, measuring out flour and water by weight (that advice I've heeded since purchasing my first electric scale fifteen years ago) and the salt, yeast, and sugar (if using) by the spoonful from their own packages into a single large bowl. No matter how I try to prevent it, inevitably, flour always gets everywhere. It dusts surfaces I had no intention of dusting. It gets into the cracks and crevices of everything. My floor inevitably looks as if a light snow has fallen when I bake. It's just as slippery as well. Several times during a baking morning, I have to wipe the bottom of my non-slip shoes with a damp paper towel to remove accumulated flour and ensure that there is friction between the bottom of the shoe and the floor.

I keep a bench scraper handy, not just for making clean cuts in bread dough but for scraping off my butcher block countertop after kneading. Because even with a light coating of flour, a thin, sticky layer still builds up. The only way to remove it, I've found, is just to scrape it off afterward.

Bits of dough manage to get everywhere. They crust the cotton towels I use to cover resting loaves. Crusty bits get lodged into the crevasses of my Danish dough hook. I've found them in the pockets of my apron and even in kitchen drawers. I'm the kind of baker who makes sure the kitchen is spotless before I so much as open a flour tin, even if I have resigned myself to the fact that I will never fully rid my kitchen of the evidence of baking. Bread just takes over.

Bread takes over the whole body. No bodily sense is not engaged on a baking day. While no-knead methods abound and many bakers flip on mixers fitted with a dough hook (including me), spending the ten minutes massaging a lump of dough into submission to develop those strand-like proteins that give bread its characteristic chew is a workout. Recently, having not kneaded dough in ages, I returned to a basic recipe for Finnish rye bread from Beatrice Ojakangas, an icon of Scandinavian baking in America and author of the James Beard Award–winning *The Great Scandinavian Baking Book*.

Ojakangas's recipe said nothing about a dough hook, and so I complied, determined to attempt this recipe word for word for a change, and kneaded for about ten minutes as instructed. I fell into a daydream where I was a contestant on *The Great British Bake Off*. It had been too long since I'd experienced the full transformation of the dough from sticky mess into smooth and pliable with my own hands. Rather than relying on sight and a few pokes as the dough was slapped around in my mixer by the dough hook, I felt a transformation in my hands up to my shoulders and back the entire time I kneaded. I could almost feel Paul Hollywood peering over my shoulder, cryptically judging my technique in silence.

I wear special recovery shoes, designed for runners, when I bake, because I know I'll be on my feet for a while. Even while a loaf rises or proves and I sit down to read or have a cup of tea, I get up regularly to check on its status, poking it to see if it springs back. I lean my face in to inhale the smell of yeast happily munching away on the sugars in the flour. I heave the large Dutch oven in and out of the oven no less than five times, first to preheat it, then to bake it in a hot and steamy microenvironment, then out again to remove the cover. Back in it goes for caramelizing the crust in the still blazing oven. And finally back out when it's finished. *If* it's finished. To check, I give it a knock on the bottom. If it sounds hollow, it's time to cool. Otherwise, it's back in the oven for a few minutes at a time. It's when the bread gets into the oven that magic starts to happen. The aroma fills my entire home. Why no one seems to sell baked bread–scented candles is beyond me. If you choose this path in life having read this chapter, then bless you.

I haven't even begun to talk about how time-consuming bread baking is. There is good reason the preferred way to get a loaf of bread home is by purchasing it at a grocery store or a bakery. Bakers will tell you that there is little *active* time, which is true. Leaving a covered bowl with bread dough in it for three days in your refrigerator is not the same as spending thirty-six hours actively cooking. Still, no recipe I've ever seen factors in the time you must spend planning a three-day bake. Or even half-day bakes. Have a doctor's appointment on your day off? How long will it take you to get there and back? What if the doctor is running late and your fifteen-minute appointment takes three hours? If you've left your dough to proof, it's going to over proof.

When I bake sourdough, I factor in a few extra days to get the starter good and going before starting on what is usually a three-day recipe, with the second day being the most time consuming. That said, baking day is a whole morning when you're baking two loaves separately (which is my only choice given that I have only one oven and only one Dutch oven).

You can't bake a loaf of bread without it taking over *everything*. Your time, your body, your space. Sure, you can dabble with a no-knead loaf here and there, but even that requires a certain level of commitment. A good no-knead loaf requires eighteen to twenty hours of rising. And try to leave the kitchen when it comes out and sings and crackles as it cools. My ears would never forgive me.

I am often confounded by the ways many Christians use or invoke Genesis, the first book of the Bible. I'm confounded by the Christians who point to Adam and Eve as if they definitively tell us something about the shape of all marriage everywhere. I'm confounded by the Christians who invoke the six days of creation as a riposte to Darwin and a guide for public school science curricula—as if the creation stories of Genesis are an explanation for how things are and should be; as if those stories are a science textbook to be read by elementary school children.

Despite my theological education, I'm not a scholar of religious history or thought and cannot tell you precisely when Genesis began to be waved in people's faces to prove a point that cannot be proven because such forms of proof are not faith at all. I can, however, tell you that a strange thing happened to faith around the eighteenth century. Faith started to become a matter of the mind. For all of the very good and very important changes in the world brought about by the Enlightenment, the early modern philosophical revolution damaged faith—it associated faith inextricably with thought. The notion "I think, therefore I am," those famous words of René Descartes, credited with laying a foundation for modern philosophy, began to infuse everything. Descartes equated existence with thinking, and it was from this principle that all things, including faith and spirituality, flowed. The mind became the locus of the person. Reason, understanding, and thought were the highest modes of being.

In the post-Enlightenment era in which we live, knowledge through the sciences is seen as the highest good. We seek understanding. But what of intuition? What of symbols that speak to us? What of eating a piece of bread for the first time and understanding it as food, not just for the body, but also for the soul?

It turns out that the brain and the rest of the body (of which the brain is a part) talk to each other. The brain is less of the command center we once thought it to be. The gut plays a much larger role than we ever realized. My intuition that food matters is affirmed with each passing study on mental, physical, and spiritual health.

Spirituality is not something other or separate from rational thought or the acceptance of scientific theories. But you won't find me wearing a shirt that says, "I believe in science," not because I reject it (I don't at all!) but because belief, to me, implies more than the mind. I don't begin my day in prayer to science, though I intellectually accept and even love the human endeavor to discover our natural world. It excites me and offers me even more material on which to contemplate the significance of life, my own and others'.

But what we can discover, know, and understand is not simply based on what we can observe through a microscope or a telescope or by a series of mathematical equations. Besides, science is a practice too. You might even say that it's a practice of faith. Faith in the possibility present in the unknown and the as yet undiscovered. Faith in the mysteries of the universe. Every experiment or study, a leap of faith that by observation we can learn more about our reality, discover patterns, and uncover truths. The scientists I know in my life don't stop practicing once they leave the lab. When my son shows a physicist friend of mine his new toys, my friend delights in the physics at work. There is something incarnational about it: the "laws" of the universe at work in a simple toy, offering a mere glimpse into something bigger.

I do believe in science. But I also believe science is a way we tell the story of who we are and why we are and what of this earth and these stars in this universe we call our home. Bake a loaf of bread and participate in the dance of faith and science. Knead dough, then let it rise in at once a leap of faith and an act of science.

Spirituality is the seeking and discovering of that certain something more to life. It asks us to use our minds and also our bodies. It is a matter of experience both of observation and of being. Spirituality is a practice, not a system of postulates and theorems. Spirituality does not offer explanation for why things are the way they are. It is not a series of rules and instructions for life that, if only followed exactly, will lead to some higher plane of being. Through disciplined practice, whether in the regular rhythm of contemplation, prayer, or even bread baking, does open worlds of wisdom and well-being.

A spiritual life is a life of practice. It is showing up for your beloved friends, lover, and community in sickness and in health, in seasons of abundance and of dearth. It is practiced in the creating and raising of another human being, a leap into the unknown if there ever was one. It is practiced in the feeding of a sourdough starter, the kneading of a dough, the slicing into a fresh-baked loaf to be shared around a table.

Spirituality reveals to others and ourselves a faith in something bigger and better, a belief in something good, whether or not that goodness is just an idea or has its source in something ineffable, divine. Either way, the only way to keep on believing is to keep on believing, which is to show up in, not just mind, but body and spirit as well. To arrive in the kitchen ready to make yet another loaf of bread.

And what a remarkable effect that showing up has. The effects of that practice get everywhere, into all the nooks and crannies of our lives, our imaginations. The birdsong in the morning suddenly sounds significant, and so you put out a feeder. An everyday loaf of sandwich bread made your kids clap their hands, and so you do it again. And again.

Whenever I need to "get out of my head," I bake bread. Moving from thinking-only mode to one that includes my arms as I push and pull dough across the counter has the power to untangle the tight knots my mind likes to wind. Inhale the scent of an active starter and I'm solving problems that have vexed me for days. Words that I could not come up with before suddenly appear. The clouds that once obscured ideas start to clear.

PRACTICE

Even after I've cleaned my kitchen after baking, dried bits of dough keep showing up. They are persistent. Under my fingernails and in my pockets. In places I didn't want. In places I did. I diligently dig the dough out of the cracks. Sweep the floor. Wash the dishes. Wipe down the countertops. And, still, I discover crumbs. I suppose I could let it frustrate me, but I'm at my best when I let it get everywhere. When I practice the assembling of ingredients into dough, the stretching and shaping of dough into bread. The clearing and cleaning of that practice. The eating of the bread. Over and over again.

FINNISH RYE BREAD

Makes 1 round loaf

Adapted from *The Great Scandinavian Bread Book* by Beatrice Ojakangas

I first learned of Beatrice Ojakangas's baking from a mention of her (and this recipe) in a baking book by Nigella Lawson. This rye bread was one of the earliest breads I ever made and one I returned to so frequently that it became expected that I would bring a loaf whenever I was invited to dinner or that I'd have one just cooled and ready when others came to sit around my table. I blame this bread for making me a baker.

Ojakangas's version of this recipe is traditional and makes two flat-ish rounds with the hole in the center, somewhat like an oversized bagel. My version makes a single loaf, cooked either on a parchment-lined baking sheet or baking stone.

2¼ teaspoons active dry yeast

1 tablespoon sugar

2 cups (201 g) warm water

1 teaspoon instant dried mashed potatoes (optional, but improves texture; you could also use leftover starchy water from cooking potatoes)

1½ teaspoons salt

2 tablespoons butter, divided

2 cups (272 grams) dark rye flour

3 to 4 cups (408 g to 544 g) bread flour

---

1. In a large bowl of a standing mixer, combine yeast, sugar, water, and instant mashed potatoes if using. Stir and let stand for 5 minutes. Add salt, 1 tablespoon of the butter, and rye flour. Beat with the paddle attachments until smooth. One cup at a time, add the bread flour, mixing on low until a dough comes together. Cover and let stand for 15 minutes to allow all the flour to hydrate.

2. Switch to the dough hook attachment and knead until smooth and pulling away from the sides of the bowl, about 6 to 8 minutes. Cover again and let rise until doubled in size, about 2 hours.

3. Lightly oil a work surface and tip the dough onto it. Knead a few times by hand and shape into a round, pulling and stretching the sides and folding in on top of itself. With both hands in a C-shape, roll it on the counter to create tension on the top.

Line a baking sheet with parchment and place the dough in the center. Cover lightly with a lightly oiled plastic wrap and allow to rise until almost doubled.

4. Preheat the oven to 375°F. Bake for 45 to 55 minutes. The bread should sound hollow when you tap it on the bottom. Immediately brush with the remaining tablespoon of butter and cool completely.

ORDINARY BREAD

IT IS A SATURDAY AFTERNOON, AND the afternoon light is streaming in through my western-facing kitchen windows. I've made breakfast and started a shrimp stock with the crispy pink shells I've saved in a zip top bag in the freezer for a month or so. My instinct to hoard for harder, leaner times and my desire for order and neatness in my decidedly not large kitchen are in a long battle. The simple shrimp bisque I plan to make for dinner is somewhat of a meeting place between the two inward pulls. It's a luxurious soup, but deceptively so. The creaminess comes from pureed rice rather than cream itself. The broth is made from squeezing the last bit of flavor from those leftover shells.

THE SACRED LIFE OF BREAD

I've tried meal plans and grocery lists and preparing lunches, breakfasts, and elements of dinner ahead of time, but all that planning feels restrictive. The kitchen is where I can find the beginnings of dinner hiding behind a Costco-size jar of mayonnaise, a half pint of leftover tomato sauce, or the last few tablespoons of frozen peas tucked inside the shelf of the freezer door. The kitchen is where I seem most able to access the thrifty resourcefulness passed on from generations of Irish women determined to feed their families with so little and the abundance and opportunity I enjoy as their descendant. The kitchen is where I feel like a magician or a witch, turning the bits and bobs from the pantry into something else entirely. I can walk to a Whole Foods, an Aldi, or a Jewel where, even stocked more sparsely thanks to pandemic-related supply shortages, I still have access to more food, both in terms of abundance and variety, than most of the world. My mother recalls always smelling turnips at her aunts' home as a child. I have access to varieties upon varieties of turnips, should I want them.

ORDINARY BREAD

For the soup, I've only had to buy more shrimp—peeled and deveined this time—and a couple of leeks. Everything else, right down to the half bulb of fennel still lingering in the crisper, I have on hand. I ponder whether we ought to have a salad or a side of some sort of vegetable. It is the dead of winter, and produce, while abundant, lacks the vibrancy that only the heat of summer can coax forth. And I'm tired of squash, sweet potatoes, and my stalwart, always-there option: frozen broccoli. I decide to skip the vegetables. The leeks and carrots in the soup will suffice. Plus, we've all taken our vitamins for the day. But we should definitely have some bread.

I check the bread box on my counter near the coffee maker. On top rest five basic varieties of salt: Maldon, Hawaiian black salt, smoked Maldon, salt gris, and fleur de sel—I simply love salt. Alas, there are only two slices of store-bought sandwich bread, and one is a heel. There are three of us who will sit down to this soup later. I'll have to make something myself. It is my day off, and I have time.

THE SACRED LIFE OF BREAD

For the past several days, I've been rebuilding the starter that I'd let go dormant in the back of the refrigerator. It had been last fed with rye flour for the last several feedings because I needed to finish a bag that had been languishing a little too long on the bottom shelf, the "cool, dry" place I store my flour. When I first opened the glass jar and stuck my nose in, I could smell pineapple and whiskey. And then excitedly ran into my husband's office to make him do the same. One should never hoard a good smell, whether from roses or rye sourdough starter.

To awaken the starter, I had to discard most of it, and so into the compost bin all but 25 grams went. Because my husband regularly brews kombucha and makes yogurt in our kitchen, wild yeasts thrive, and therefore reviving my starter never takes very long. If I plan to bake bread within the week, I can build back my starter within about four or five days. I'm an amateur, however, and I'm interested in a manageable bread baking process that doesn't involve gymnastics-like antics to get an active starter. This is just the process that works for me, producing flavorful loaves in my own kitchen with less work than it would take to walk to the store to buy a loaf at the grocery store bakery and considerably less work (and money) than I'd have to expend to get to one of the good bakeries nearby (that are all closed on Monday—my day off—and Tuesday anyway).

I've been in the kitchen for hours already. Before the shrimp stock, I made a lemon poppy seed cake, inspired by the slow marathon of one episode a night of *Great British Bake Off* I've been watching with my son. But we need bread. I *want* bread. And I want it from my own hands. But I don't have the two days to get the tangy sourdough loaves I would normally bake, so I opt for something I consider a little more ordinary and decide to make something more quick-rising, a sort of blend between sourdough and sandwich bread, using a pinch of yeast to assist the starter.

The result is something crusty and chewy, sturdy enough for dipping into the bisque, soft enough that it absorbs the soup like a sponge.

THE SACRED LIFE OF BREAD

We never eat quietly but with conversation that twists and turns depending on who is talking. We sigh in appreciation for this ordinary bread, with satisfaction for another extraordinary meal.

If these chapters have anything to offer it is that bread is anything but ordinary. We often modify *bread* with the adjective *simple*, a nod to its often unadorned qualities. But to call it so is to conceal the days of measuring and mixing, kneading with your hands, your arms, your whole body. To call it ordinary risks ignoring the life of the grain that came to be the flour. It looks away from the life of the soil in which that grain grew. It does not acknowledge how that mysterious blend of water, salt, yeast, and flour become more than the sum of its parts but something synonymous with life itself.

I often think about how Western Europe was divided for centuries, in part over ideas of what a piece of bread could and couldn't do. Yes, there was more at stake than theology in the Reformation, but at the heart of many divisions were arguments about the power bread had to be

God or point to God in the world. Before the Reformation, the Western and Eastern churches were split on what kind of bread to break at the table, leavened or unleavened. Even today, families experience divisions over who can and who cannot receive bread in a ritual in which it is blessed, broken, and shared. I think of my own wedding, where we chose not to break bread in the wedding ceremony because I knew half of the guests wouldn't. I told myself that the reception was enough, but I've always regretted that we couldn't share in a meal of Holy Communion.

Because I am a woman, there are members of my own church who will not receive bread that I have blessed with my own hands as a priest. When I baked communion bread for my kid's baptism, I had family members abstain as well, not because the ceremony wasn't in a Catholic church but because the priest was a woman and the assisting priest gay. Still I longed for them to experience the sharing of bread as something powerful in and of itself, no matter the gender or identity of who called it powerful.

THE SACRED LIFE OF BREAD

We can call bread ordinary all we want, but even before it is ritualized, blessed, and consecrated to become something else, bread is something extraordinary. It holds within its crust the story of life and death and life again. In its crumb structure is a tale of creation alive even when we cannot see it. In its flavor, time-earned wisdom. In its crunch and chew, the nearness of comfort. You don't have to be a cradle Catholic or an Episcopalian with a pronounced piety around bread to know that bread is a source of transformation. Bread is used in a vast variety of religious customs all around the world. You don't have to think anything about Jesus or organized religion at all.

Bread belongs to us all, whether we're deeply religious, agnostically searching, or just appreciate discovering the more there is to life. And that is extraordinary.

PECAN CINNAMON SNAILS

Adapted from Beatrice Ojakangas

Makes 24 snails

Viennoiserie, a style of baking associated with croissants and Danish, refers to baked goods leavened by yeast and made ultra-flakey by laminating, or sealing, butter between layers of dough. Most people don't bother to bake in this style at home because of the amount of time it takes and difficulty getting perfect, shattering layers. This recipe uses a method that makes homemade Viennoiserie (Viennabrød in Danish) somewhat more accessible.

It is still quite time consuming but much more forgiving than traditional laminating techniques.

I include this recipe, because, like all Viennoiserie, there is no mistaking that it is extraordinary bread. Sweet and crispy, these snails are best consumed the day they are made, preferably still warm from the oven. It makes 24 snails, which means you should probably have people over if you're going to make them. They taste even better in the company of others.

Pastry

3½ to 4 cups all-purpose flour
1½ cups chilled unsalted butter
2 packets active dry yeast
½ cup warm water

ORDINARY BREAD

½ cup heavy cream

½ teaspoon freshly crushed cardamom seeds

½ teaspoon salt

2 eggs, room temperature

¼ cup sugar

Filling

½ cup butter, softened

1 cup brown sugar (light or dark)

1 cup finely chopped pecans

1 teaspoon cinnamon

¼ teaspoon salt

Icing

---

1 cup powdered sugar

3 to 4 teaspoons hot coffee

---

1. In a food processor, pulse together 3½ cups
    flour with butter cut into ¼-inch slices until
    the butter is about the size of kidney beans.
    You can also cut the butter into the flour
    using a pastry blender. The food processor is
    so much faster.

2. In a large bowl, proof the yeast in warm water
    for 5 minutes. Once it is bubbly and foamy on
    top, stir in the cream, cardamom, salt, eggs, and
    sugar. Add the flour-butter mixture to the bowl
    and stir together, just until the dry ingredients
    are all moistened. Cover and refrigerate for at
    least 4 hours, but preferably overnight.

3. Generously flour a large workspace. I usually
    use my dining room table. Turn the dough
    out onto it and lightly flour the top. Roll
    the dough out into a 16- by 20-inch square.
    Fold the dough into thirds along the long
    edge. Turn it around and roll it out again
    and fold into thirds, making a perfect square.
    Chill for 30 minutes and then repeat again.
    Refrigerate.

4. Prepare two muffin tins with 24 paper liners.

5. Remove the dough from the refrigerator and roll out into a 20-inch square. Working quickly to keep the dough from softening, spread with the softened butter, being sure to get it all the way to the edges. In a small bowl, combine the brown sugar, pecans, cinnamon, and salt. Sprinkle this mixture over the top of the butter. Starting on one side, roll up the dough creating one long log with a spiral inside. Cut 24 equal slices, and place them cut-side up into the muffin tins.

6. Allow the snails to rise slightly in a cool place, about 30 to 45 minutes. Then cover with plastic wrap and refrigerate overnight.

7. The next day, preheat the oven to 375°F. Beat 1 egg and brush over the tops of the snails. Bake until golden, 20 to 25 minutes.

8. Before the snails come out, whisk together hot coffee and powdered sugar until smooth. Drizzle over the snails while hot. Serve warm.

ACKNOWLEDGMENTS

I AM INCREDIBLY GRATEFUL TO LIL Copan and the entire team at Broadleaf Books for steering me through the writing of my first book with such patience and encouragement. Thank you to Lil for cheering me on from the moment I sent you my idea and for continuing to have faith in it even when I had lost mine.

I am indebted to the inimitable Lauren Winner for her honesty and wisdom about how to write as myself, an Episcopal priest, without preaching. Thank you for wondering with me about what I needed to say and what I didn't.

Thank you to Heidi Haverkamp, Teri Ott, Celeste Kennel-Shank, Melissa Early, and Elizabeth Felicetti. Writing with you every Thursday

237

morning is a highlight of my week. You keep me accountable but always with good humor and grace. My gratitude goes especially to Heidi for inviting me years ago to write with this incredible group of women and for initiating an introduction to Lil well before I decided to write this book.

To Kelly O'Connor McNees, for your persistent reassurance that I could do this and that everything I experienced writing my first book was normal (and even more so in a pandemic, with a full-time job, and with a young kid who couldn't go to school).

Thank you to Harold and Jill at Janie's Mill for an exquisite day at your farm and mill (and Celia for baking a loaf of bread that was my first taste of Black Emmer, now a favorite grain of mine to bake with).

Thank you to all my friends and family who cheered me on during what ended up being the wildest year or so of my life and for keeping me grounded in your friendship and love: Steve, Nadia, Erika, Catherine, Kathryn, Bridget, Chris,

ACKNOWLEDGMENTS

Cate, Jeremy, Dave, Charlie, Malia, John, Sarah, Mom, Dad, Maria, David, and Susan.

To all the professional bakers who turn out loaves (and croissants and scones) that I buy regularly to inspire my own baking, especially Lost Larson in Chicago and Hewn in Evanston.

And finally, to Andrew and Albie, for your faith in me and for eating all the bread (when you finally could). You are the leaven to my life.

Ingram Content Group UK Ltd.
Milton Keynes UK
UKHW040755060623
422736UK00008B/20/J